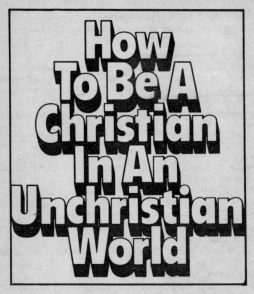

How To Be A Christian In An Unchristian World

Fritz Ridenour

Illustrator: Joyce Thimsen

Editorial Research: Georgiana Walker

Regal Books

A Division of GL Publications
Ventura, CA U.S.A.

Other good reading:

How to Be Happy No Matter What by Tom Watson, Jr.
Will the Real Phony Please Stand Up? by Ethel Barrett
Here Comes Jesus by Ed Stewart
Counterfeits at Your Door by James Bjornstad

The translation of all Regal books is under the direction of GLINT. GLINT provides technical help for the adaptation, translation and publishing of books for millions of people worldwide. For information regarding translation contact: GLINT, P.O. Box 6688, Ventura, California 93006.

Translations and versions of the Bible used in this book are designated by the following superior letters:

a *The New American Standard Bible.* © The Lockman Foundation 1960, 1962, 1963, 1968, 1971, 1972, 1973, 1975. Used by permission.

b *The Living Bible,* Copyright © 1971 by Tyndale House Publishers, Wheaton, Illinois. Used by permission.

c *THE NEW TESTAMENT IN MODERN ENGLISH,* Revised Edition, J.B. Phillips, Translator. © J.B. Phillips, 1958, 1960, 1972. Used by permission of Macmillan Publishing Co., Inc.

d *Good News Bible,* The Bible in Today's English Version. Old Testament copyright © American Bible Society 1966. New Testament copyright © American Bible Society 1966, 1971, 1976. Used by permission.

e *Revised Standard Version* of the Bible, copyrighted 1946 and 1952 by the Division of Christian Education of the NCCC, U.S.A., and used by permission.

f *Authorized King James Version.*

Eighteenth Printing, 1983

Published by Regal Books
A Division of GL Publications
Ventura, California 93006
Printed in U.S.A.

Library of Congress Catalog Card No. 72-169603
ISBN 0-8307-0611-9

CONTENTS

A Teacher's Manual and Student Discovery Guide
for Bible study groups using this book are available
from your church supplier.

82074

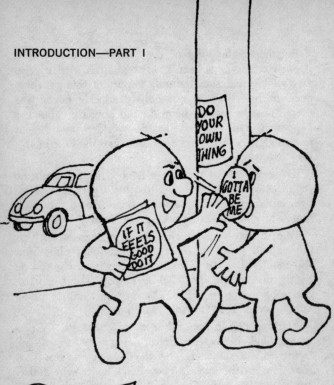

POP! GOES EXISTENTIALISM

According to folk singer Johnny Cash, the lonely voice of youth wants to know, "What Is Truth?" When it comes to defining "Truth" everyone seems to have his own answer, but no one has *the* answer. Philosophers have been seeking truth for thousands of years. Their conclusion: *there is no truth*—at least not in an absolute sense. At best, *all truth is relative.*

Reigning philosophy of the twentieth century is a popularized form of secular existentialism, that cynical view of life that says the only important thing is existence—to *be*.* God is not only dead, He never was there. There's nobody home in the universe. Man has happened into a lonely hostile world where life is meaningless, absurd and he must make the best of this very bad joke.

The existentialist says there is no objective truth, no set of standards with final authority. Every man is his own authority. Every man turns out his own value system as he goes about the business of "being."

Due to plays, novels and books by men like Albert Camus and Jean-Paul Sartre, the ten-dollar philosophical mouthful called existentialism has been chewed on by the masses and spat back as a "pop" point of view. It even has its own slogan, already something of a contemporary cliche: "Do your own thing!"

You find pop existentialism in today's songs, TV programs, films, books, magazines, newspapers. People are trying to act debonair and devil-may-care, but they have fear in their eyes. They don't know where they are going because they don't remember where they started and they're not sure what their destination should be.

The first six chapters of this book seek to help you:

. . . Understand how secular man thinks . . . why he says there is no absolute truth anywhere . . . why he has sold out to a new morality that is no morality . . . why he'd rather do his own thing than do the right thing.

*The above description deals with secular or atheistic existentialism. Originating with the Danish theologian Soren Kierkegaard in the nineteenth century, existentialism split into two branches—secular and theological. See chapter 6.

. . . Determine how today's Christian thinks . . . **or** should think if he is willing to take the Bible seriously.

. . . Discover why the Christian claim to absolute truth is valid and how to communicate this validity to a secular society heavily influenced by atheistic existential ideas—no objective truths . . . no final authority . . . life is meaningless . . . a big joke and we all have to make the best of it.

You can do more than "make the best of it," and one brief letter in the New Testament will tell you how.

While in prison at Rome in A.D. 62, the apostle Paul heard of how Christians in the church at Colosse were

3

being swayed by heretical philosophies that claimed Christ was something less than God. Paul responded by telling them that in Christ, Christians have everything. Christ is the whole truth. There is no one else and there is nothing more. Christ is not to be apologized for, explained in a way that makes Him palatable to modern minds, or watered down into an insipid set of ethical rules.

Paul's words to first century Colosse are even more relevant for today's believer. Paul tells it like it *must be* . . . through Christ, and *only* through Him, you can learn how to be a Christian in an unchristian world.

CHAPTER 1

CHRIST IS THE ANSWER
What is the question?

The message was painted in huge letters on the subway wall "Christ is the answer." And underneath, as a put on (or perhaps a put-down?), someone had scrawled: "What is the question?"

This dialogue in graffiti illustrates the attitude that much of the secular world holds toward Christianity: it's all right as a religion, but it's irrelevant for real life in the twentieth century.

A prime example would be Vicki Stevens, who was a confirmed agnostic when she enrolled as a freshman at the University of California at Berkeley. Vicki had attended confirmation class in her church, but stopped believing in God while in high school.

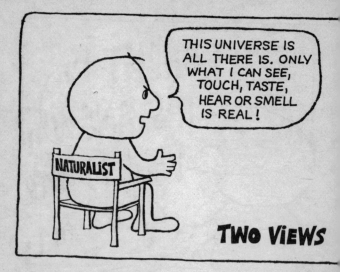

TWO VIEWS

"At times I attended church to please my parents but it meant nothing," Vicki explains. "No great incident destroyed my faith, it was something I grew out of, like the belief in Santa Claus: a comforting myth, nice to believe, but unfortunately it did not fit the facts of life.

"When I came to 'Cal' my agnostic suspicions were crystallized and reinforced by intellectual arguments. Anthropology, psychology, sociology all seemed to agree that the concept of a personal God was a figment of man's imagination. Having seen no evidence to the contrary I put the subject of God out of my mind."

Vicki's case was hardly unique. Most people are products of a public school education that stresses the scientific approach and empirical experience. Truth is what you can measure, what you can "prove for sure."

Behind this secular viewpoint is the basic assumption that this universe is really all there is. C. S. Lewis calls

6

OF TRUTH

this the *Naturalist* view. Naturalists, says Lewis, believe ". . . that the ultimate fact, the thing you can't go behind, is a vast process in space and time which *is going on of its own accord.*"[1]

Theologian Francis Schaeffer illustrates the difference between the secular and Christian view by asking you to imagine two men sitting in a room. Imagine that the room is all there is to the entire universe. There is nothing outside and all that is inside are the two men sitting on two chairs. One man holds the Naturalist viewpoint.* For him, the universe consists of nothing but mass, energy and motion. The other man is a Supernaturalist. He is a Christian who believes in the Bible as the revelation of God.

*In his illustration Schaeffer uses the term *Materialist,* which in this context means the same as Naturalist—one who thinks the universe is made up of nothing but what he can see, taste, feel, touch and hear.

The Naturalist decides he will explore the one-room universe and he does so, producing a tremendous number of books which describe everything in the room—even the particles of paint on the wall. The Naturalist asks the Christian what he thinks of all of his books and upon examining them, the Christian replies, "A tremendous amount of work but it's incomplete."

"What did I miss?" the Naturalist wants to know. And the Christian tells him he has another book, the Bible, which talks about the Supernatural—something the Naturalist didn't put in his books.

The Naturalist can't believe his ears and tells the Christian that he is insane. The Christian tells the Naturalist that he's the one who is a little off, because he's only talking about part of his own universe.

For the Christian there is more to the universe than what can be seen, handled and analyzed. The Supernatural part is that something beyond nature—outside of it. Dr. Schaeffer points out that the word *Supernatural* is not the best one to describe the unseen portion (although it is often used). For the Supernaturalist, says Schaeffer, the unseen portion of the universe is just as "natural" as what can be seen.

Schaeffer stresses that these two views—Naturalist and Supernaturalist—are diametrically opposed. One is right and one is wrong and there is no compromise.[2]

If the Christian can get the point from Dr. Schaeffer's illustration, he will find college, military service or just life in general a lot easier to operate in. Of course, there aren't just two people in the universe; there are billions. The universe is a lot bigger than one room and there is more in it than a couple of chairs and paint on the wall. But the Naturalists of the world are in the same boat as the Naturalist in the illustration. Their world is made up of mass, energy and motion. They refuse to admit there is something else—the unseen—the

8

Supernatural, *which created the natural from outside.**

Naturalists, agnostics, secularists, materialists all claim that Christianity "doesn't fit the facts of life." They refuse to admit any Supernatural power outside of nature which has created nature and which can interfere in nature if it (He) so wishes.

On the other hand, Christians say that life has meaning because of the Supernatural, because God created life and sustains it. In addition, God has revealed Himself to men. First through His dealings with His chosen people, the Jews (recorded in the Old Testament) and then, through the sending of His Son into the world to become a human being, live here among us, die for our sins and rise again from the dead.

In a way, Christianity is the only truly Supernatural religion. No other religion makes claims about its founder like the claims Christians make about Christ.

Naturalism allows a God 'within nature'

As C. S. Lewis points out, the difference between Naturalism and Supernaturalism is not the difference between belief in God and disbelief. Naturalism, says Lewis, could admit a certain kind of "god" — a great cosmic consciousness coming out of nature itself. Naturalists do not object to this kind of god because he does not stand outside of nature or the total system and does not exist on his own. Nature is still "the whole show"—the basic fact—and such a god is merely one of the things which the basic fact contains. What Naturalism cannot accept, stresses Lewis, is the idea of a

---

*Granted, there's a lot of talk today about supernatural occult practices and beliefs (astrology, witchcraft, spiritism, etc.), but in the context of this chapter I am speaking of Supernaturalism with a capital *S*. As C. S. Lewis points out in his book, *Miracles* (chapter 2), the word *Supernatural* refers to one God—the creator of the universe from the outside.

personal God who stands outside Nature and made it.[3]

The Scriptures say God *does* stand outside of nature, that He did make it, and that He invaded it to bring men back to Himself after they had strayed from Him through sin. What Christianity is really all about is precisely the difference between Naturalism and Supernaturalism. Almost half of the New Testament was written by the apostle Paul in the form of letters to new Christian churches in cities like Ephesus, Rome, Colosse, etc. In these letters, Paul explains again and again just what Christians really have in Jesus Christ and why Christ is God's final and complete revelation of Himself to men.

A prime example is Paul's letter to the church at Colosse. The church there was being taken over by a group of intellectuals who decided to rewrite the Gospel to suit their philosophical ideas. Some of these intellectuals were Jewish legalists and others were Greeks who were teaching a system of thought that would come to be known as Gnosticism.

The Gnostic heretics of the Colossian church were saying that Christ wasn't divine, definitely not equal with God the Father. They stressed the philosophical point of view—meaning human wisdom. They were willing to talk about God but they wanted to keep Him in the realm of a principle or an idea rather than a person who would send His Son to die for man's sins and rise again from the dead.

Paul had never been to Colosse, which was located in the Lycus Valley, about one hundred miles due east of Ephesus in Asia Minor (Turkey today). Paul had not started the church in Colosse nor the churches in neighboring towns like Hierapolis or Laodicea. But he knew of them, and when he received word that heresy was in their midst, he had to try to help. He couldn't go to Colosse personally because he was in prison in

Rome at the time. So he wrote his letter—addressed to Colosse but meant also for the Christian churches in Hierapolis and Laodicea nearby.

How would you begin a letter to straighten out confused believers whom you've never met? Coming on strong and bawling out the brethren for backsliding wouldn't help much. Instead, Paul is optimistic and encouraging . . .

"FROM: Paul, chosen by God to be Jesus Christ's messenger, and from Brother Timothy. TO: The faithful Christian brothers—God's people—in the city of Colosse. May God our Father shower you with blessings and fill you with His great peace.

"Whenever we pray for you we always begin by giving thanks to God the Father of our Lord Jesus Christ, for we have heard how much you trust the Lord, and how much you love His people. And you are looking forward to the joys of heaven, and have been ever since the Gospel first was preached to you.

"The same Good News that came to you is going out all over the world and changing lives everywhere, just as it changed yours that very first day you heard it and understood about God's great kindness to sinners. Epaphras, our much-loved fellow worker, was the one who brought you this Good News. He is Jesus Christ's faithful slave, here to help us in your place. And he is the one who has told us about the great love for others which the Holy Spirit has given you.

"So ever since we first heard about you we have kept on praying and asking God to help you understand what He wants you to do; asking Him to make you wise about spiritual things; . . . that the way you live will always please the Lord and honor Him, so that you will always be doing good, kind things for others, while all the time you are learning to know God better and better.

11

We are praying, too, that you will be filled with His mighty, glorious strength so that you can keep going no matter what happens—always full of the joy of the Lord'" (Col. 1:1-11).

You have to give Paul credit. He is optimistic and positive. True, there was a core group of faithful believers in the Colossian church, but there also had to be plenty of brethren who were full of confusion, doubt and even rebellion. For all Paul knew, the real believers at Colosse may have been in the minority. People have a way of following the crowd, and the Gnostics were articulate enough to get quite a few people to follow them.

But in his opening sentences Paul doesn't water down his personal philosophy. God is the *Father* and Jesus Christ is *His Son*. The Gospel is still Good News that says you can reach heaven through faith in Christ. The Gospel says that you can have hope in a world where there doesn't seem to be much hope. Furthermore, Christ can change your life, full of sin as it might be.

Notice that Paul doesn't spend any time "proving the existence of God." Paul knows that it does little good to argue about that. No one can prove God is really there or not there. Even philosopher Bertrand Russell, arch-enemy of Christianity and all religions, admitted that he could not prove that God did not exist.[4]

But the Christian doesn't try to prove God's existence. He puts his faith in the highly credible evidence found in Biblical revelation. More precisely, he puts his faith in Christ, who is God's supreme revelation of Himself. Because of Jesus Christ he can know God's love and peace, plus the joy of heaven. As Paul put it in his letter to Colosse, the Christian is . . .

". . . thankful to the Father who has made us fit to share all the wonderful things that belong to those who

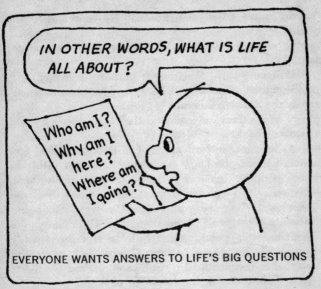

EVERYONE WANTS ANSWERS TO LIFE'S BIG QUESTIONS

live in the kingdom of light. For He has rescued us out of the darkness and gloom of Satan's kingdom and brought us into the kingdom of His dear Son, Who bought our freedom with His blood and forgave us all our sins'"b (Col. 1:12-14).

The last half of the twentieth century is what might be called the super-paradox of all time. People are smarter than ever and in more trouble than ever. Philosophies like humanism say we are getting better and better but even a casual glance at the newspaper labels this claim naive.

We have learned (or are learning) the answers to many questions—everything from how to send men into outer space to how to design custom-made human beings through genetic surgery. Technologically speaking, we have a lot of information and we are getting more all the time. But secular man still can't answer satisfactorily basic questions that life continues to ask us all:

Who am I? (Where did I come from? What is my origin?)

Why am I here? (What is my purpose for living?)

Where am I going? (What is my destiny—my potential for success or failure?)

If you wanted to combine the three questions into one, you could ask: *"What is life all about?"*

As an agnostic freshman at Cal Berkeley, Vicki Stevens thought she knew the answer. She was sitting in the Naturalist's chair. For her, God wasn't really there. He was just a figment of man's imagination—or so she thought. When she was assigned a term paper and asked to compare existentialism with Christianity, she felt comfortable and familiar with the atheistic views of Jean-Paul Sartre and Albert Camus. But when she started to talk about Christianity she realized she didn't have a clear idea of the philosophy of Christ.

"All I could remember from Sunday School," recalls Vicki, "was 'love your neighbor as yourself.' Not only did I become aware of a gap in my intellectual knowledge; for the first time it appeared I had rejected a philosophy which I did not understand."

Vicki finished her term paper, but Christ was not finished with her. A few weeks later, Campus Crusade for Christ representatives spoke at Vicki's sorority. That first meeting led to others with the wife of the Campus Crusade director and soon they were discussing Christianity over coffee once a week. The Campus Crusade worker kept saying that Christianity was not a religion but a relationship with a Person, Jesus Christ.

Vicki had to admit that the Biblical perspective hung together. That is, it was consistent and made sense as long as you went along with its basic assumption, the existence of a Supernatural yet personal God. But Vicki couldn't buy that. She was still sitting in the Naturalist's chair, unwilling or afraid to admit that the Supernatural God was really there and could affect her life.

On a cloudy cold Easter Sunday, Vicki got on the plane to fly back to Berkeley after spending her Spring quarter vacation at home in Pasadena. The plane took off in a blanket of storm clouds and then broke through the gloom into blazing sunlight. At that moment, Vicki got out of the Naturalist's chair. It seemed as though God had said to her: "I Am."

"I realized one could stand down in the airport all his life, looking up, never knowing that the sun was shining behind the clouds. That the sun was giving life to everything on the planet. It seemed that the Bible had given me some pieces of the God puzzle, but because I did not have all the pieces, I had been saying that God did not exist. Now I saw how limited my intellect was, how ridiculous it was to fathom the infinite with a finite mind."

Before her plane landed in San Francisco Vicki made a simple turnover of her life to Christ. She said, "All right, Jesus, I give myself totally to you. Do whatever you want to with me."[5]

Vicki is one of the thousands, actually millions, who have experienced Jesus Christ as the answer. Increasing numbers are finding Him to be the answer today, because as never before, people desperately want to know what life is all about: Who am I? Why am I here? Where am I going?

There are two ways to approach these questions—from the Naturalist's chair or the Supernaturalist's chair. From the Naturalist's chair, these questions lead to a dead end. From the Supernaturalist's chair, these questions lead to what Paul is talking about in the opening paragraphs of his letter to the Colossians.

There is no need to go through life not knowing who

you really are, where you are going, and what you are supposed to be doing while on the way. Those who sit in the Christian Supernaturalist's chair know exactly who they are: creations of God and His spiritual children (see John 1:1-14). As for where he is going, the Christian knows his ultimate destination is eternal life with his heavenly Father (John 3:1-16). As for what he is supposed to be doing with his life, the Christian has the general directive from Christ to love God and love his neighbor as himself (Matt. 22:30-40).

Granted, these broad answers to life's tough questions don't cover every specific situation and problem the Christian faces. But the Christian can work out specific problems and questions as he trusts in and relies on Jesus Christ—God Himself.

Until Christ came, most religions were 'guesses at God.' Even Judaism, the faith in which Paul was reared, was still an incomplete picture. But in Christ the guesswork and incompleteness are ended. If you sit in the Supernaturalist's chair of the Christian you may not have "all the answers" but you have *the* answer to the questions that ultimately matter: Who am I? Why am I here? Where am I going?

Christ really is the answer. He is the truth. He is the way. He is what life is all about. He is God and He is really there!

FROM WHERE YOU SIT

According to this chapter, what is the key difference between the Naturalist and the Supernaturalist?

When some Naturalists talk about "God," are they referring to someone outside of the universe who made "this whole show" or do they mean something else?

When considering what it means to be a Christian (Supernaturalist) in an unchristian (Naturalist) world, why are *presuppositions* (from where you start your thinking) important?

The Supernatural point of view . . .

Read Col. 1:1-14 in as many versions as possible, especially *The Living Bible*. Compare it with Eph. 1:1-14. How does Paul see man? Do his statements indicate that man is alone in the universe?

Compare what Paul says in these passages from Colossians and Ephesians with Christ's Words in Matt. 6:25-34, and John 14:1-3, 15-19. Do you think it is a cop-out to trust God to "take care of your tomorrow" (Matt. 6:34)? Do you think it is a weakness to take comfort in knowing that Christ has prepared a place for you (John 14:2)? Why or why not?

If you'd like to do some further reading . . .

Death in the City, Francis Schaeffer, Inter-Varsity Press, 1969, especially chapter 9: "The Universe and Two Chairs."

Miracles, C. S. Lewis, Macmillan, 1963, particularly chapters 1-7, which deal with the difference between Naturalism and Supernaturalism.

Basic Christianity, John Stott, Inter-Varsity Press, 1957. See especially the preface and chapter 1, "The Right Approach," which spell out the difference between Naturalist and Supernaturalist views.

Your God Is Too Small, J. B. Phillips, Macmillan Company, 1961. After disposing of inadequate misconceptions of God, which are based on Naturalist views and ideas, Phillips goes on in Part 2 to focus on an adequate (Supernatural) God.

Quotes worth considering . . .

"If Naturalism is true, 'I ought' is the same sort of statement as 'I itch' or 'I'm going to be sick . . .' In a world of Naturalists (if Naturalists really remember their philosophy at school) the only sensible reply would be 'Oh, you are, are you?' All moral judgments would be statements about the speakers' feelings mistaken by him for statements about something else (the real moral quality of actions) which does not exist. —C.S. Lewis.[6]

Don't just sit there . . .

Try interviewing different people, Christian and non-Christian, friends and strangers, and get their answers to the questions: Who am I? Where am I going? Why am I here? Are their basic presuppositions based on Naturalism or Supernaturalism?

CHAPTER 2

Jesus loves me...

So WHAT?

Jesus loves me! This I know,
For the Bible tells me so.
Little ones to Him belong;
They are weak but He is strong.

"Jesus Loves Me" is probably the first song a lot of Sunday School kids learn to sing. And when you're four and five years old, singing "Jesus Loves Me" with a smiling, motherly kind of teacher is fun. It makes you feel good—kind of warm and secure.

But ten to fifteen years (or so) later "Jesus Loves Me" doesn't provide quite as much comfort. By then this little kindergarten song about what "the Bible

19

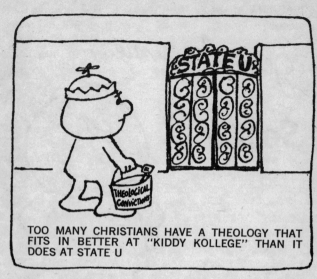

TOO MANY CHRISTIANS HAVE A THEOLOGY THAT FITS IN BETTER AT "KIDDY KOLLEGE" THAN IT DOES AT STATE U

tells me" may seem like a tea bag that spent too much time in hot water. For some Christians, the Bible doesn't seem to have much zip.

As one student at a Christian college put it: "I can't remember when I had a 'quiet time,' as they talk about here, and I'll tell you frankly I don't know a sharp kid on campus who does. We get the Bible in chapel, and the required Bible courses, and sure, all this is part of my thinking and shapes my frame-of-reference in many ways, but so far as thinking of the Bible as something personal and vital in my life, I don't."[1]

In effect, this student—and there are many others like him—is saying, "Yes, Jesus loves me, but so what? I believe all the doctrines. I accept the Bible as true, but it doesn't seem to do very much for me where I really live."

Perhaps there's a clue in the first verse of "Jesus

20

Loves Me." It reads, "Little ones tc Him belong; they are weak but He is strong." Could it be that too many Christians come up through the Sunday School and the church getting the idea that Jesus is only for little ones, but when they become men and women they must put away "childish things"?

Could it be that every year thousands of Christians graduate from high school and head for college campuses casually carrying a kindergarten concept of Christianity instead of a mature experiential faith in the God-man from Galilee? Could it be that as far as real understanding and real convictions about Jesus Christ are concerned the churches are turning out young people (and plenty of adults) who have a theology that fits in better at "Kiddy Kollege" than it does at State U.?

When it comes to who Jesus Christ really is, people have been confused (or have been trying to confuse others) for almost two thousand years. No sooner had Jesus risen from the dead and ascended into heaven than there were those who started saying He hadn't done any of these things at all, that He wasn't divine, that He was a phantom in human form, etc., etc.

All this heresy set Paul to thinking and the result was one of the greatest passages in all Scripture:

"Christ is the exact likeness of the unseen God. He existed before God made anything at all, and, in fact, Christ Himself is the Creator who made everything in heaven and earth, the things we can see and the things we can't; the spirit world with its kings and kingdoms, its rulers and authorities; all were made by Christ for His own use and glory. He was before all else began and it is His power that holds everything together.

"He is the Head of the body made up of His people —that is, His church—which He began; and He is the Leader of all those who arise from the dead, so that He is first in everything; for God wanted all of Himself to be in His Son.

"It was through what His Son did that God cleared a path for everything to come to Him—all things in heaven and on earth—for Christ's death on the cross has made peace with God for all by His blood. This includes you who were once so far away from God. You were His enemies and hated Him and were separated from Him by your evil thoughts and actions, yet now He has brought you back as His friends.

"He has done this through the death on the cross of His own human body, and now as a result Christ has brought you into the very presence of God, and you are standing there before Him with nothing left against you—nothing left that He could even chide you for; the only condition is that you fully believe the Truth, standing in it steadfast and firm, strong in the Lord, convinced of the Good News that Jesus died for you, and never shifting from trusting Him to save you. This is the wonderful news that came to each of you and is now spreading all over the world. And I, Paul, have the joy of telling it to others"[b] (Col. 1:15-23).

To the Gnostics with love—Paul

Paul writes these mind-bending thoughts about Christ with a specific purpose. He wants to help people who are being swayed and influenced by Gnostic ideas. Although the great formal systems of Gnosticism were not developed until the second and third centuries, there were plenty of Gnostic ideas around in the first century when Paul wrote his letter to the Colossian church.

Gnosticism was a mixed bag of philosophical tricks and its ideas came from mythologies of Greece, Egypt, Persia and India. When the Gnostics found out about

Christianity they thought they could work some of its doctrines into their pagan teachings.

The Gnostics got their name from the Greek word *gnosis* which means "knowledge." Gnostics liked to claim they had a secret inside track on knowing about God (their idea of God anyway). So, in Colosse and other Christian churches they were doing their best to turn Christianity into a philosophy that was intellectually respectable. (Somehow this all has a familiar ring. There are still plenty of people—some of whom are supposedly in the Christian fold—who want to turn Christianity into a philosophy that is "intellectually respectable.")

Gnostics taught that only the spirit was good and that all matter was evil. They also believed that matter was eternal and that the world had been created by what they called a "demi-urge," a thirtieth or fortieth-rate god who was far enough away from the Real Thing to be allowed to touch filthy matter.

According to Gnostic theories, Christ was just one more creature created by this demi-urge. And to keep things confusing, they also taught that Jesus of Nazareth was sort of a spook in carpenter's clothing who didn't leave footprints in the dust of Palestine's roads. Another weird Gnostic idea was that a "heavenly Christ" took possession of the human man, Jesus, but before the Crucifixion this heavenly Christ left Jesus and only a man died on the cross.

So, by the time the Gnostics got through with Him, Jesus was far less than God. Jesus' life and teachings were only part of the big picture that the Gnostics felt you needed to rise to spiritual heights according to their system.

In Col. 1:15-23 Paul sets out to deliberately refute Gnostic theories about Christ. To answer Gnostic claims that Christ was a created creature, Paul replies

by saying that Christ is the image of the invisible God
—His exact likeness. How can something *invisible* have
an *image?* Bible scholar Bernard Ramm illustrates the
concept by pointing out that electrons and atomic particles are essentially invisible but these atomic particles
can be photographed on sensitive photographic plates
or as they are discharged into liquid nitrogen.

"In each instance," says Ramm, "we do not literally
see the atomic particle but we see an image of it. And
so no man sees the very nature or essence of God, but
the nature and essence of God is reflected in Christ,
His Son incarnate, and in Christ we therefore have the
most perfect knowledge of God, His nature, purposes
and intentions that is possible for man to have. *No religious philosophy can compete with this!*"[2]

Paul goes on to say Christ was there before God
made anything at all and in fact, Christ Himself is the
one who made it all (Col. 1:15,16).*

In the next verses Paul continues to make claims for
Christ never heard before. Not only did Christ exist before all else began but He holds everything together.
(See Col. 1:17 and compare it with Paul's speech to the
philosophers on Mars Hill in Acts 17 where he talks
about the God in whom all men live and move and
have their being.)

In a final slap at Gnostic gobbledygook, Paul says
God wanted all of Himself to be in His Son (Col.
1:19[b]). Jesus wasn't a phantom. He wasn't a human
being possessed by some sort of heavenly spirit. *He
was fully God and fully man.* He had to be. No mere

---

*The Greek text put it, "The firstborn of all creation," which
sounds as though Christ was the first thing God created. Jehovah's
Witnesses like to interpret the verse this way. Actually, "The firstborn of all creation" is the title of honor and has nothing to do
with timing. In his commentary on Colossians Bible scholar
William Barclay says, "We may translate the phrase: 'He was
begotten before all creation.' "

RECONCILIATION WAS GOD'S IDEA, NOT MAN'S . . .

human could have carried out His assignment—the reconciliation of God and man. (See Luke 19:10; II Cor. 5:19.)

Reconciliation is a heavy theological term, but there are earthly analogies to help explain it. We speak of an estranged husband and wife being reconciled or having a reconciliation. Friends have reconciliations. So do groups who have been arguing or fighting with one another.

But there is one important distinction when you talk about the reconciling work of Christ. Christ reconciled men to God. He did not reconcile God with men. In other words, *man's* attitude needed changing, not God's.

Sometimes we seem to get the idea that God was full of wrath and retribution, just waiting to clobber everyone for sin and disobedience. And so, when Jesus reconciled God and men, He supposedly changed God's mind as much as He changed men's minds. The Bible doesn't teach this. God initiated the whole procedure. Reconciliation was *His* idea. He loved the world enough to send Christ in the first place (John 3:16). Through Christ, He reconciled (brought back) the world to Himself (II Cor. 5:19).[3]

Reconciliation is what Paul is talking about in Col. 1:20. Through Christ's death on the cross, God cleared a path for everyone to come to Him.

The cross and Christ's death are not pleasant ideas. They are not attractive ideas but they are necessary ideas. Note that Paul says in Col. 1:21 that *we* were God's enemies and hated God. *We* were separated from Him with *our* evil thoughts and actions but it is God who brought *us* back to Him and there *we* stand, sinners but with nothing against *us*.

It's as if God was saying, "If my son's death on the cross does not melt your hard hearts then nothing will, outside of my forcing you to return to me." But God doesn't force us because God is love and love does not force others to love in return. That would be slavery and would result in hate, not love.

But there are conditions to God's offer. We must realize what it means to be lost in sin. We must repent and turn from sin to Christ and want to go the other way. We must fully believe the Truth—Christ who died for *us* (Col. 1:23).

Do Paul's ideas jibe with Jesus' words?

At this point you may be asking an obvious question: "Where did Paul get all these ideas?" Was he writing his own version of a spiritual philosophy in order to argue with people who didn't agree with him? Or, does what Paul says jibe with what Jesus said about Himself and what other apostles wrote about Jesus? You can go back to the Gospels and check for yourself. Again and again, Jesus made claims of deity. Just two of many examples are John 10:30 ("I and the Father are one") and John 14:9 ("Anyone who has seen Me has seen the Father!").*

During the three years of His public ministry, Jesus taught with authority that went far beyond the human level. He didn't ask people to believe His Words but to believe in *Him* (John 6:27-29).

Again and again the Pharisees—the religious leaders of the Jews—got so angry with what He said that they wanted to kill Him for blasphemy (for claiming that He was God). For examples, see John 5,7, or 8.

C. S. Lewis, the great writer of Christian apologetics at the popular level, observes that it is unlikely Jesus' followers were the kind of men who would be easily convinced by His claims. Jesus' first followers were Jews and if the Jews were convinced of anything it was that there was only *one* God. There couldn't possibly be two or more. But Jesus didn't go around saying, "You have a God in heaven and I'm God, too," Instead He said, "I and the Father are one." This wasn't easy for Jesus' own disciples (Jews) to believe. It took the Resurrection, plus the power and witness of the Holy Spirit, to finally convince them.

Lewis also points out that if Jesus had been only a man who was a "great moral teacher," His many claims to deity would have made Him sound like a candidate for the funny farm. Lewis says:

"There is no half-way house, and there is no parallel in other religions. If you had gone to Buddha and asked, 'Are you the son of Bramah?' he would have

*For other passages in which Christ implies or claims deity, see John 14:6; Matt. 28:19,20; Mark 14:61,62. For what other apostles thought of Jesus, see Peter's words in Matt. 16:16,17 and Thomas's confession of faith in John 20:25-28.

said, 'You are still in the veil of illusion.' If you had
gone to Socrates and asked, 'Are you Zeus?' he would
have laughed at you. If you had gone to Mohammed
and asked, 'Are you Allah?' he would first have rent his
clothes and then cut your head off. If you had asked
Confucius, 'Are you heaven?' I think he probably
would have replied: 'Remarks which are not in accordance with nature are in bad taste.' The idea of a great
moral teacher saying what Christ said is out of the
question. In my opinion, the only person who can say
that sort of thing is either God or a complete lunatic
suffering from that form of delusion which undermines
the whole mind of man. . . .'"

Like Paul, but in different words, Lewis also pin-
points the difference between the Naturalist and the
Supernaturalist. The Naturalist wants to keep Jesus on
the human level where He is easier to handle. Jesus the
man isn't particularly disturbing or threatening. He's a
good teacher whose sayings you can accept or reject,

OF JESUS

depending on how relevant and practical they seem to you for twentieth-century living. But you remain captain of your soul and master of your fate.

In the fall of 1970, Decca Records published a rock opera, *Jesus Christ Superstar,* written by two young Englishmen, Andrew Webber and Tim Rice. A tongue in cheek put-down on Supernatural Christianity, the album describes Jesus as a "superstar" teacher and healer who spoiled it all by getting a messianic complex.

Interestingly enough, while Webber and Rice apparently deny Christ's deity, their rock opera seems to leave the question of Jesus' true identity wide open. After he betrays Jesus, Judas (who is presented as a sort of hero), is engulfed in remorse and wonders about Jesus' strange power. Jesus is just a man, but, says Judas, "He scares me so."

On the way to Golgotha, the crowd wants to know who Jesus is. What has He sacrificed? Does He think that He is who people have been saying He is—God?

Even "convinced Naturalists" who write rock operas seem to be fascinated by the possibilities of the Supernatural. Could it be that God is *really there?* Could it be that He came in the Person of Jesus Christ—Superstar?

The New Testament answers with a resounding YES! In Col. 1:15-23 Paul fairly shouts, "Jesus does love you and look what He has done for you."

A lot of people grow up in the church saying they believe Jesus loves them and that He died for them. But all too many of them seem to become Christians without learning what it means to be Christians in an unchristian world. They go off to college, boot camp or car pools taking them to their first job and what happens? At the bidding of brilliant professors, with-it roommates, or swinger friends and acquaintances the "scales drop from their eyes." Some of them chuck Christianity altogether. Others relegate their faith to a file called "less important." Many others go through the motions but are not quite sure why they bother.

How come?

Is "Yes, Jesus loves me" strictly an idea for kindergartners? Or is it that too many Christians get faked out of position by Naturalists because they don't know where they really stand as Christian Supernaturalists? They do not realize that a great shift in the concept of truth has taken place due to the work of the pragmatists, the idealists, and many other Naturalist-based philosophers. (See chapter 5.)

That is why the tendency on the typical college campus is to see Jesus Christ "as a possible way to find the truth." He isn't attacked outright as a liar and a fraud. He is simply added to the lists of great performers and teachers. It's much more in fashion to praise Christianity as "socially useful."

30

We ALL walk by faith . . .

There are secular professors who will pat the Christian on the back and congratulate him because he finds his faith personally satisfying. And in the same breath they say almost sadly, "If you have faith in Christianity, keep it, but it's not for me."

The message comes through loud and clear. The professor is really telling the Christian, "I have outgrown all that, my boy, and I am a man come of age. I don't need any crutch called God and what you really need to do is plumb the depths of the universe. Admit that man can't count on anything but himself and his own efforts. He is alone. Existence is a bad joke and he must make the best of it. Yet he must ever seek knowledge and realize that the truth is unknowable in its final sense."

This kind of line makes perfectly good sense— *if you want to start with Naturalist presuppositions* (that this world is all that there is). But there is no law that says you have to. The man who sits in the Naturalist's chair appears intelligent, debonair, suave, sophisticated— worldly-wise. And he may well be all these things— particularly worldly-wise. But the Naturalist sits in his chair by faith just as the Supernaturalist sits in his chair by faith. If you start from the Supernaturalist's chair then you know Christ is not "a way to find truth." He is *The Truth*. He is, in modern vernacular, the whole bag; He is holding the whole show together.

Whenever you talk about getting at the truth you usually mean that you want to get to the bottom of things, or get to the heart of the matter.

In the first chapter of Colossians, Paul is saying that Christ is at the bottom of things. He is the foundation. He is the very One who created the world. He is the Head of His Body (those who believe in Him). Proof of

31

this for finite minds is His resurrection from the dead.

All of God is in His Son Jesus Christ and it was through His Son that God made it possible for man to know Him—The Truth. Jesus, the man, and Christ, the eternal God, are one Person. To be a Christian is to personally encounter this Person experientially, in a way that matters, in a way that changes your whole outlook on life—what you do and say and think.

"Yes, Jesus loves me" is not a "so what?" idea. It is not agreeing to a string of conservative doctrines. It is not swallowing some kind of fundamental creed without chewing on the meaning of the words.

Read Col. 1:15-23 over and over again. Commit it to memory. Think it through. And then you will see "Yes, Jesus loves me" is *everything* . . . because He is The Truth!

FROM WHERE YOU SIT

What do you think? Is "Jesus loves me" an idea for kindergarten kids or is it for *you*, too. Why or why not?

In your opinion just who is Jesus Christ? Try and go beyond the usual one or two-word pat answers. How many facts can you list about Him after reading this chapter?

Do you agree that a lot of Christian young people go to college as easy targets for secular arguments that destroy their faith? In what way does Col. 1:15-23 pinpoint the difference between a Naturalist point of view and a Supernaturalist point of view?

The Supernatural point of view . . .

Reread Col. 1:15-23 and list in your own words the claims that Paul makes about Christ. Does what Paul says jibe with what Jesus said about Himself and what other apostles wrote about Jesus? To check, see Christ's own words in John 10:30; 14:9; Luke 2:49; Matt. 28:19-20; Mark 14:61,62; John 14:6. Also, see what Peter and Thomas say about Christ in Matt. 16:16,17 and John 20:25-28.

Compare Col. 1:15-23 with John 15:9,13; Rom. 8:35-38; Gal. 2:20; I John 3:16. Then write a brief paragraph on what "Jesus loves me" means to you.

If you'd like to do some further reading . . .

Mere Christianity, C. S. Lewis, Macmillan, 1964, especially Book II, "What Christians Believe" and Book IV, "Beyond Personality: Or First Steps in the Doctrine of the Trinity," some of the best reasoning concerning the Supernatural Person of Christ available to the layman.

Basic Christianity, John Stott, Inter-Varsity Press, 1957. See especially Section 1 on Christ's Person and Section 3 on Christ's work.

Christ the Controversialist, John Stott, Inter-Varsity Press, 1970. See especially Stott's introductory essays, "A Defense of Theological Definition" and "A Plea for Evangelical Christianity." Also see chapter 1, "Religion: Natural or Supernatural?"; Also see chapter 4, "Salvation: Merit or Mercy?" and the postscript, "Jesus, Teacher and Lord."

Quotes worth considering . . .

"Essentially Christianity is Christ. The Person and work of Christ are the foundation rock upon which the Christian religion is built. If He is not who He said He was, and if He didn't do what He had said He had come to do, the whole super-structure of Christianity crumbles in ruins to the ground."—John Stott[5]

"Had this doctrine of the divinity of Christ been lost, Christianity would have vanished like a dream."—Thomas Carlyle[6]

Don't just sit there . . .

Talk to several people this week, Christian and non-Christian, and get their ideas on "Who is Jesus Christ?" (See how many Christians can name facts about Christ that are in Col. 1:15-23.) Write a letter to someone and explain just who Jesus really is as you understand it from Col. 1:15-23. (If possible, actually send your letter to someone you know; but whether you send it or not, writing your thoughts down will show you just how much you do understand about Christ.)

Memorize Col. 1:15-23. The *Living Bible* paraphrase is good.

Arrange with two or three friends to listen to the rock opera, *Jesus Christ Superstar*. Analyze what it is saying. Is it done from a Naturalist or Supernaturalist point of view? Does it make you angry? Sad? Thoughtful?

CHAPTER 3

THe WhoLe TRuTh AND NoThiNG BuT tHe TRuTh?

Bill came from a dedicated Christian family. Among other things his father was a deacon, Sunday School teacher, young people's advisor. His mother was a choir member, VBS superintendent plus holder of numerous other church jobs. Bill grew up watching Mom and Dad put their Christianity into action—or at least into activities.

As a young boy, Bill believed in Christ as his Saviour and faithfully practiced his parents' moral code. Kids at high school who swore, smoked and drank were off-limits for Bill. He liked his church group and Christian camps. Throughout high school Bill was secure in church activities and his church's ideas on morality and standards.

And then Bill went to college.

The first semester saw him living with fellows who had different behavior patterns, different ways of looking at things. Unlike Bill, they didn't cherish a personal faith in God, they didn't attend church much and they had different ideas about personal habits and sex.

Bill's psychology and sociology professors looked at things differently too. They tried to sound objective but seemed to work from basic underlying assumptions that included the innate goodness of human nature, man is getting better and better, science is the only way to truth.

In the dorm bull sessions, everybody was cool and wanted to ask "significant questions." Nobody tried to come to definite conclusions. After all, "truth is always relative."

Bill noticed that a lot of his fellow students would finally make some decisions or value-judgments and they seemed to base them on what the group thought or perhaps it was their inner desires.

Your God is just a father image . . .

Bill tried to explain his behavioral code but his dorm-mates couldn't see how a list of dos and don'ts had anything to do with faith in Christ. They told Bill his God was sort of a father-image to reinforce the code he had been taught. But to really rely on God? That was a psychological crutch for immature people who couldn't handle life.

And of course they brought up the standard questions: Does God exist? What about the heathen? Can sincere Buddhists be wrong? What about evil?

Bill couldn't answer their questions. But he didn't give up his faith or his moral code. He got involved in Bible study, prayer meetings, and found a church to attend. His religious activities kept him feeling secure and accepted. He didn't have to justify himself at every turn.

At the end of his freshman year, Bill moved in with a Christian friend. Now he had real relief from agnostic arguments and pressures to conform to non-Christian codes. Bill had little contact with non-Christians after that, except for attending classes.

Bill didn't witness much but he did pray for the conversion of non-Christians on campus. Now and then he would run into old dorm-mates and try to invite them to Bible study but they never accepted. Bill didn't really think they would. They knew where he stood and wanted no part of God.

Occasionally, Bill had doubts about his faith. He tried to get rid of them by thinking about the faithfulness of his parents, his Christian friends, etc. But his interest in Christianity started to fade.

The summer after his sophomore year, Bill was really disillusioned. He just couldn't get excited about Christianity anymore. Yes, he knew Christ had died for his sins. Bill prayed every day and he knew his Bible—promises of salvation, verses on the abundant life, those grim words on eternal judgment for unbelief. Yes, Bill knew all that but it didn't seem to tie in with his life and his plans. He wanted a career, a nice home and family—the whole bit.

Bill's Christianity seemed like a Pepsi without the fizz. All the life had gone out of those values that had seemed so important back in high school. Bill was tired of the old choruses. And, for him, standard Christian phrases—the Lord's will, trust in the Lord, my sins are covered, prayer changes things—started sounding like pious clichés. Bill felt like a diseased tree. On the outside he looked firm and upright enough, but inside he felt hollow and rotting. Inside he kept asking: "How can I say I know 'the truth'?"[1]

HOW DO YOU KEEP THE FIZZ?

Does Bill sound real or imaginary? Maybe you know a Bill. Maybe *you* are Bill, or maybe you are well on your way to becoming just like him. Bill is a typical "head-knowledge Christian." Yes, he felt strongly about Christ but he went to college with more doctrines and ideas than real dynamics in his life.

Bill had tried to make it all work but he finally folded, not so much shot down as worn out. So the question looms large: How *do* you keep the fizz in your Christian life? How do you communicate the Bible's explicit claim to THE TRUTH? According to the Scripture, Christ is *the only Way, the only Truth, the only Life.* (See John 14:6; Acts 4:12.)

That's a rather incredible claim to make to a secular society that gets up-tight if anyone tries to go beyond the generally understood rule that all truth is relative. After all, everyone has "some truth." No one has all the truth. Having all the answers is impossible. It's hard enough to know if you're asking the right questions.

The apostle Paul had the same problem—communicating the absolute truth of the Gospel to a skeptical society. Yet his letters crackle with conviction that Jesus is *The Truth*—no other way needed.

Paul explains just why a Christian can (and must) say he has *all* the truth in Christ . . .

"But part of my work is to suffer for you; and I am glad, for I am helping to finish up the remainder of Christ's sufferings for His body, the church. God has sent me to help His church and to tell His secret plan to you Gentiles. He has kept this secret for centuries and generations past, but now at last it has pleased Him to tell it to those who love Him and live for Him, and the riches and glory of His plan are for you Gentiles too. And this is the secret: *that Christ in your hearts is your only hope of glory.*

"So everywhere we go we talk about Christ to all who will listen, warning them and teaching them as well as we know how. We want to be able to present each one to God, perfect because of what Christ has done for each of them. This is my work, and I can do it only because Christ's mighty energy is at work within me"[b] (Col. 1:24-29).

In verse 24, Paul brings up an uncomfortable idea. Living as a Christian in an unchristian world involves suffering. In fact, Paul feels that he is finishing up the remainder of Christ's sufferings for His church. This doesn't mean that Christ needed any help to pay the full penalty for sin. But it does mean that as the Christian serves Christ and shares Him with others, he should expect some suffering, sacrifice and pain. In an unchristian world, painless Christianity is a contradiction, and it also loses its fizz.

And so how do you keep fizz in your Christian life? Paul tells you the secret in Col. 1:25-29. The secret is to have Christ in your heart. That line is practically a cliché, but what it means is that doctrines won't produce any reality or power in your life. Neither will behavioral codes or lots of church activities. All these things are good but they are the *results* of a personal relationship with Jesus Christ. Your personal relationship with Christ is your *source* of spiritual power. Without the Holy Spirit everything else is so much ecclesiastical toothpaste.

If you do not have this personal relationship with Jesus, you can easily get sucked into the "all truth is relative" game that is so popular in today's secular society, particularly on the college campus. For example, a non-Christian asks you the question, "How can you prove there is a God?" And so, immediately you try to prove it. You do this because you've been reared in an atmosphere where right answers are very important. You must have the specific, minutely precise solution to everything in order to substantiate your faith. The trouble is, a lot of your precise answers come from the Bible—a book that people don't necessarily believe is true.

So how do you handle sticky questions?

For example, there is always the fellow who is ready to tell you that God is your psychological crutch. He says you believe in God because you can't handle reality. Of course, if God really *is* your psychological crutch, you just might get up-tight and defensive. On the other hand, you could point out to the other person that this crutch accusation is *his* psychological smoke screen. He doesn't really want to admit the possibility of a Creator who has made him because then he would owe his allegiance and service to that Creator. And, of course, if he admitted that God was his Creator it would follow that God would hardly be his crutch.

Of course, you can take a completely different approach. Go ahead and admit that in a way God is your "crutch." Then ask, "And who isn't limping?"

Another smoke-screen kind of question is, "Would a just God condemn the heathen to hell just because they haven't heard of Christ?" This approach gets the spotlight off what the non-Christian really thinks about God and can make the Christian start feeling as though he is part of an unfair conspiracy against a sizable chunk of the human race. There isn't any need to fall into this trap, but remember to make conversation, not points for your side of the argument.

For one thing, you can say that you believe God is a just God and whatever He does with people who never heard will be fair. Secondly, as you understand it people don't get condemned because they never heard of Jesus Christ. They are condemned because they violate their own moral standard. Every race across the face of the earth has this moral standard as Romans 3 clearly points out and the science of anthropology concurs.

Don't forget to bring the conversation back where it belongs—on the subject of Jesus Christ. The Bible is clear that no one is saved apart from Christ. The real issue isn't what is going to happen to the heathen. The real issue is what each one of us does with Jesus Christ and His claim to authority in our lives.

Another basic question along the same lines, "How can you claim that Christianity is the only way to God?" What about all the other great religions of the earth? Can't these people get to God in their own particular way?

THE MAJORITY OF INTELLIGENT PEOPLE DO NOT BELIEVE THE BIBLE FOR THE SAME REASON THAT THE MAJORITY OF NOT SO INTELLIGENT PEOPLE DO NOT BELIEVE IT . . .

Don't sputter around trying to explain away almost 500 million Mohammedans, plus millions and millions of Buddhists and Hindus. It doesn't hurt to admit that morally and ethically many of the great religions of the world are similar to Christianity. Buddhism, for example, has its eight-fold path which is a great deal like the Ten Commandments.

But the real point is that Christianity is faith in Jesus Christ, not in the teachings of a man who got a certain kind of religious enlightenment (for example, Mohammed or Buddha). No other religion claims that its founder was God Himself, that He paid the price for man's sin and guilt, that He rose from the dead. The deity of Jesus Christ (that He was God come to this planet) is the unique claim of Christianity.

42

Because millions of people embrace other faiths does not disprove the Bible's revelation. If Christ is who He said He was, He is the *only* real answer to man's sin— the only way to God. You don't arrive at the truth about God by voting on it nor by counting to see whose religion has the most followers. If something is true it's true, and no number of votes to the contrary is going to change it.

Some people like to point out that the majority of intelligent people do not believe the Bible. But that's an easy one. The majority of intelligent people do not believe the Bible for the same reason that the majority of not-so-intelligent people do not believe: it makes too big a moral and ethical demand.[2]

In other words, the Bible cramps their style. Humans are strange paradoxes. We all want peace, happiness, fair play, justice, freedom, yet we constantly deny ourselves these things because of our own hang-ups. The battles rage within us. If we would turn ourselves over to God, our Creator, and follow His pattern for life, take His value system, *then* we would have peace, happiness, joy, etc. But we don't really want to do this. We want to do things *our way*, and that applies to many believers as well as nonbelievers.

Unfortunately, too many Christians operate on what seem to be the chains of religious slavery—legalistic codes and rules. They are only practicing a religion called Christianity; they are not experiencing spiritual freedom and release through personal experience of Christ.

And here we come right back to Bill, reared in a fine Christian home, an enthusiastic participant in church activities during his youth. But when Bill hit college he found that Christian knowledge and even Christian activities are not the same as Christian convictions and experience.

THE CHRISTIAN CAN'T SIT IN BOTH CHAIRS

Bill had the answers but *he never learned the secret.* Paul says that God's secret plan is there for all to know and that plan is Christ Himself (Col. 1:26,27). If you have Christ in your heart you have hope—power for life. Christ is why you can say you have The Truth.

Christianity—if left a religious or philosophical system—soon runs out of fizz. Keep your Christianity at a philosophical or strictly religious level and people will rip it apart. That's what happened to Bill.

But if you bring Christ into the picture, it puts the fizz back into everything. Obviously then, the question is, "What do you mean bring Christ into the picture and put fizz back into everything?"

Perhaps it helps to come back to those two chairs. Could it be that a lot of Christians say they are Supernaturalists but they are living like Naturalists? Could that have been Bill's real problem? Bill knew all the answers, but they turned out to be mostly theory. When he got away from his nice safe church surroundings and into the secular world, he became another casualty Christian. He retreated from the attacks of his materialist-minded dorm-mates and tried to pull a shell of religious activities and interests around himself. But what finally got to him was the enemy within—his own heart, which was centered more on Naturalist and materialist goals and values than on Christ.

Christianity with fizz in it is strictly a Supernaturalist affair. The Bible says the Christian can be in Christ and Christ can be in him giving him hope and power.

But in a way it is dangerous to "have the truth in Christ." You have to let Christ work in your life. If you don't—if you keep Christ cooped up in your head like a theory or a system—your Christian life becomes stagnant, flat and tasteless.

The Christian has work to do. He has purpose for life—to share his life with Christ and then share Christ with others. Paul sums it up in Col. 1:28,29: "So everywhere we go we talk about Christ to all who will listen . . . . This is my work, and I can do it only because Christ's mighty energy is at work within me."[b]

FROM WHERE YOU SIT

According to this chapter how can the Christian avoid getting sucked into playing the game of "proving his faith is true"? Is the key having all the answers?

What do you recall from this chapter that would help you answer the charge: "God is your crutch"?

What do you recall from this chapter that would help answer questions about the heathen being condemned to hell because they haven't heard of Christ?

What do you recall from this chapter to help you answer the questions, "How can you claim that Christianity is the only way to God? What about the other great religions?"

Why do many intelligent people fail to believe the Bible?

The Supernatural point of view . . .

Colossians 1:24 and 25 talk about Christ's sufferings and how Paul believes that he is completing Christ's sufferings. Is this mention of sufferings an isolated reference or is suffering truly part of being a Christian in an unchristian world? Check Rom. 8:17; II Cor. 1:7; Phil. 3:10.

What did Christ say about suffering in Matt. 5:11; 10:22; 10:39?

In Col. 1:26-29 Paul talks about God's great secret which is Christ in you, your hope of glory. How does this match up with what Christ taught in John 14:12-27 or John 15:1-11?

What is the key to allowing Christ's mighty energy to work within you? See Rom. 8:1-11; Gal. 5:16-23.

If you'd like to do some further reading . . .

How to Give Away Your Faith, Paul Little, Inter-Varsity Press, 1966. The entire book is good but see especially chapter 4, "What Is Our Message?" and chapter 5, "Why We Believe."

Mere Christianity, C. S. Lewis, Macmillan Company, 1964. Perhaps the best brief work on Christian apologetics available. See especially Book I, "Right and Wrong Is a Clue to the Meaning of the Universe," and Book II, "What Christians Believe."

Know Why You Believe, Paul Little, Inter-Varsity

Press, 1968. Excellent discussion of typical sticky questions Christians need to think through.

Quotes worth considering . . .

"We need to be reminded that ultimately man's basic problem is not intellectual; it is moral. Once in a while our answer won't satisfy someone. His rejection of the answer doesn't invalidate it. On the other hand, he may not be convinced and still not become a Christian. I've had fellows tell me, 'You've answered every one of my questions to my satisfaction.' After thanking them for the flattery I've asked, 'Are you going to become a Christian then?' And they've smiled a little sheepishly, 'Well, no.' 'Why not?' I've inquired. 'Frankly, it would mean too radical a change in my way of life.' Many people are not prepared to let anyone else, including God, run their lives. It's not that they can't believe; but they *won't* believe."—Paul Little[3]

Don't just sit there . . .

List the sticky questions about Christianity that are hardest for you to deal with. Then, deliberately seek to talk about these questions—with Christian friends and then with non-Christians.

CHAPTER 4

CAN YOU PUT THE
TRUTH IN A BOOK?

In a world that claims there are no absolutes, a book that comes on with as much absolute authority as does the Bible can get short shrift indeed. For example, the following capsule review ran in the campus newspaper at a large university in the United States:

The Bible, by God, Moses, Paul and various and assorted prophets. This highly inspired work, although prodigious in moral philosophy, variety of characters and optimism, falls short in its plotting. The action appears to move backward as much as it moves forward, and the hero dies in the middle. Although pervaded by symbolism all the symbols are bleedingly obvious; which means all the gods and goddesses will flock to give them different interpretations when the book reaches the public's attention. A must for bedtime reading. Recommend seeing the movie.[1]

This kind of tongue-in-cheek sacrilege is typical of the sophisticated secularist, and it can be hard on

48

Christians who come from a Christian background to the agnostic university setting. As one Christian who went to a secular college puts it:

"In my own church everyone assumes that the Bible is God's Word from cover to cover but here at the university my trust in the Bible is always under fire. Since my church didn't give me any reasons for belief in inspiration, it seems to me that now I have to give up faith in the Bible if I'm intellectually honest."[2]

This Christian student is in the standard dilemma. He is sitting in the Supernaturalist's chair (discussed in chapters 1 through 3), but most of those around him are not. Most of his college professors and classmates appear to be Naturalists or materialists—at least as far as the Bible is concerned.

As chapter 1 pointed out, there are a lot of people who are willing to admit, "Oh, I suppose there's a God of some kind . . ." but when it comes to accepting *revelation* from God, they back away. At heart they are Naturalists and cannot believe that there is Someone outside of the universe who has communicated with mankind in a book. Furthermore they are suspicious or downright hostile toward the idea that a certain book can pack so much authority, so many absolute pronouncements.

When the collegian quoted above mentions, "Nobody gave me any reasons why the Bible is inspired," he voiced a feeling that is in a lot of Christians. God's basic *plan* built around Jesus Christ and His love sounds great. But how do they define the *blueprint* that spells that plan out—namely the Scriptures of the Old and New Testaments?

Strangely enough, Paul never mentions the "inspiration of Scripture" in the book of Colossians. He is too busy talking about Jesus Christ. When it comes to sorting out your feelings and convictions on the authority of the Bible, perhaps Jesus Christ is the best place to start. Too many people try to start at the other end: they want to be sure the Bible is "completely true" and *then* they will consider Jesus Christ. But when Paul heard about the Gnostic heresy in the church at Colosse he didn't send in a long defense of the Scriptures. He didn't call the Scriptures "final truth." He called Jesus Christ the final truth. For example:

"I wish you could know how much I have struggled in prayer for you and for the church at Laodicea, and for my many other friends who have never known me personally. This is what I have asked of God for you: that you will be encouraged and knit together by strong ties of love, and that you will have the rich experience of knowing Christ with real certainty and clear understanding. *For God's secret plan, now at last made known, is Christ Himself.* In Him lie hidden all the mighty, untapped treasures of wisdom and knowledge"[b] (Col. 2:1-3).

In this passage and in the entire book of Colossians, Paul is emphasizing that final truth and knowledge rests in Christ. Christians owe their trust, allegiance and faith to their Lord and Saviour. He has the final authority in their lives.

If you can buy that basic premise, you can buy the inspiration and authority of Scripture for a very simple reason. The Reverend John R. Stott, one of today's leading Bible scholars, got at the real issue while talking to Wheaton College students in a chapel meeting:

"We believe that the Bible is the Word of God because our loyalty to Jesus Christ requires us to do so. We believe that His authority and the Bible's authority stand or fall together."[3]

The reason Stott says this is because Christ endorsed the authority and the inspiration of the Old Testament (and the New Testament too, although it wasn't written yet).

Jesus admitted to the authority of the Old Testament Scriptures again and again. For example, He said, "The Scripture . . . cannot be untrue"ᵇ (John 10:35).

When Satan tempted Him in the wilderness, Jesus always answered the devil by quoting Scripture as the final authority for His decisions and His actions (see Matt. 4:1-11 or Luke 4:1-12).

In His many debates with the religious leaders of His day, Jesus always went to the Scriptures as the final source of right or wrong. He told the Sadducees, "You are wrong, because you know neither the scriptures nor the power of God"ᵉ (Matt. 22:29). He confronted the Pharisees with their real problem when He said, "For the sake of your tradition, you have made void the word of God"ᵉ (Matt. 15:6).

John Stott points out that although Jesus was the Son of God, He voluntarily chose to submit humbly to what Scripture said. If it was "written in Scripture," that was good enough to settle the issue for Him. *

Even a casual reading of the Gospels shows that Jesus endorsed the Old Testament many times, but what about the New Testament, which wasn't written yet? John Stott observes that Jesus endorsed the New Testament by commissioning His apostles to write it. According to Stott, the Greek word *apostolos* means "deputy" or "delegate." It means that you speak and teach in the name of the person and authority of the person who has sent you. Jesus chose the original twelve. He called them *apostoloi*. In effect He said, "He who hears you, hears Me. He who receives you,

*Stott emphasized this point in his Wheaton College chapel address. For a further excellent discussion on the authority of Scripture and what Christ thought of Scripture, see Stott's book, *Christ, the Controversialist*, chapters 2 and 3, Inter-Varsity Press, Copyright 1970.

51

AWFULLY MORALISTIC...
GOOD BEDTIME READING
I GUESS... MAYBE I'LL
SEE THE MOVIE...

NATURALIST

TWO VIEWS

receives Me. He who rejects you, rejects Me." (See Matt. 10:40.)

Jesus trained His apostles for three years and then just before His death He promised them the inspiration of the Holy Spirit. (See John, chapters 14, 15 and 16.) Later Saul of Tarsus was chosen as an apostle in a dramatic encounter on the road to Damascus (Acts 9).

Stott says, "The apostles were unique in their personal authorization by Jesus Christ, in the eyewitness experience of Jesus Christ, and in their extraordinary inspiration by the Holy Spirit. If you want to bow to the authority of Christ you must bow to the authority of the apostles because He commissioned then to teach in His name."[4]

If you claim to sit in the Christian's Supernaturalist chair, you not only accept God's plan but His blueprint as well. Jesus is your Lord and Saviour. He died for your sins and rose again from the dead—all part of God's *plan*. And Jesus believed, practiced and endorsed

OF THE BiBLE

the entire Bible as the inspired Word of God—the *blueprint*. If you say you want to follow Christ, you must, by simple logic, agree with what He says about Scripture.

When Paul says God's secret plan is Christ Himself (Col. 2:2) he isn't making philosophical small talk. He knows that human theories are a dime a dozen. But what Christ did on the cross cost God everything. Paul isn't spouting philosophical theories. He is reminding the Colossian Christians of facts—the Gospel—history that really happened.

Truth for Paul is the Person Jesus Christ. Paul knew that God had broken into history in Christ, who lived among men, died for their sins and arose from the dead.

The New Testament is an eyewitness report of what God did in and for the world in the Person of Jesus Christ, His Son. And the Christian has no trouble calling this eyewitness report trustworthy, authoritative and inspired because the Christian assumes that God is really there and that the Supernatural view of the world is a very live option.

You always have to come back to those two chairs—Supernaturalist or Naturalist. The Christian Supernaturalist believes God created the world. It follows that man can't get along without his Creator. God is not an idea, a religious prop, a psychological crutch for sniveling neurotics. God is *really there*. He has spoken in His Son and the Bible is the inspired record.

Bible apologist Edward John Carnell has observed that what separates the Christian and the critics of Scripture is not the facts of Scripture but *two different philosophies of reality*.[5] The Naturalist can't buy the Bible because the Bible mentions things that go beyond the Naturalist's concept of reality.

There are people of course who aren't sure if they are Supernaturalists or Naturalists. They sort of stand around on one agnostic foot or the other trying to decide. Rob Witmer's story is a good example of this kind of indecision. While at Wheaton College he began asking himself if it were logical to believe in God. If God did not exist he might as well live the way he wanted instead of trying to follow a narrow Protestant ethical standard.

But then Rob remembered the many times he had faced death and had called upon God to help him. And what about all those times he had taken God's name in vain? If God did not exist, why use His name at all? Why think about Him and talk about Him? Where did people get this idea of God anyway?

He decided to examine Christianity and . . .

Rob Witmer decided to examine Christianity more carefully. Was the Bible the revelation of God? He didn't know. He never had read the Bible cover to cover and because the New Testament was easier to understand he started with that. He says:

"While reading the Gospel of Matthew, I realized that I had many misconceptions about God. I saw how good Christ was in different situations. I gradually realized that God was speaking to me through that book. I decided that I did believe what Matthew had written about Christ. At this time, I totally submitted my will to God's Will. I prayed a simple prayer like this: 'God, I realize that I have done many things that are wrong. Please forgive me, because I believe that Christ is your Son. I now agree to follow your Will instead of my will. Everything that I am and have is under your control. Thank you.' God then gave me the power to build my life the way I wanted. I can now honestly say that I know Who God is."

There's something important in what Rob Witmer says and if you miss it you miss the whole point about what Christians mean by an inspired Bible. He didn't read every last word of the New Testament, check it out for every possible inconsistency, discrepancy, etc., decide that it was totally one-hundred percent accurate and *then* believe what Matthew had written. He came to the Bible willing to admit that God could really be there (a Supernatural view). Then he let the Bible speak.

When Rob made his decision he trusted Christ as the Son of God and his Saviour from sin. He didn't pray to an inspired Bible to save him.

In short, Rob Witmer examined an eyewitness account by one of the apostles and accepted the evidence. He did not put the Bible through some kind of higher critical computer to make sure that it was accurate to the final detail.

To put it in words of Dr. Kenneth Kantzer, Dean

of Trinity Theological Seminary, "The Christian doesn't insist that one must believe *everything* in the Bible before he is convinced of *anything* in it."[6]

The Christian has many reasons to believe that the Bible is inspired, but the best reason is Jesus Christ Himself. The Naturalist may take his potshots at the Christian faith and the Scriptures but he still has to contend with the evidence. The Resurrection reports in the New Testament have never been proven false. Various critics of Scripture and Christianity have advanced their theories to explain away the Resurrection but their theories remain theories in the face of eyewitness accounts, the authenticity and authority of which have never been refuted.*

Can you put The Truth in a book? Yes and no.

If you look on the Bible as the object of your faith (and surprisingly a lot of Christians do just this) you make the Bible a "paper Pope." As John Stott says, "Many people have too 'low' a view of Scripture; they do not accept it (as Jesus did) as the written Word of God. At the same time, there are others whose view of Scripture is too 'high.' They regard Scripture with an almost supersititious reverence. They become so absorbed in Scripture itself that they lose sight of its purpose, which is to manifest Christ to them. They earn for themselves the title 'bibliolater' or 'Bible-worshipper,' for they behave as if Scripture and not Christ were the object of their devotion."[7]

Ironically, when you make the Bible your object of

---

*For a recent example of trying to explain away the Resurrection, see *The Passover Plot*, Hugh J. Schonfield, published by Bernard Geis. Copyright 1966. Schonfield's description of Christ makes the crucifixon a carefully staged execution—a pseudo death arranged by a man who had carefully studied the Old Testament to discover what he would have to do to convince the Jews that he was their Messiah. For an excellent discussion on the authority and authenticity of the New Testament, see *The New Testament Documents, Are They Reliable?*, F. F. Bruce.

IF YOU WORSHIP THE BIBLE INSTEAD OF CHRIST, YOU PLAY THE NATURALIST'S GAME.

worship, you play the Naturalist's game. You wind up worshiping paper and ink rather than trusting in the fact that the Bible is God's Supernatural revelation. The Bible teaches, reports and reveals The Truth. In this sense it is God's inspired blueprint. But God's secret plan is Jesus Christ. It is Christ who saves and *in Christ* lies all wisdom and knowledge!

FROM WHERE YOU SIT

What do you think about the chapter's claim that Jesus Christ has final authority? If you say you are a Christian, does Jesus Christ have final authority in your life? Do you really agree with John Stott when he says: "We believe that the Bible is the Word of God because our Lord Jesus Christ requires us to do so. We believe that His authority and the Bible's authority stand or fall together"?

Can you think of three Scriptural examples of where

Christ endorsed the authority and inspiration of Scripture? In what way did he endorse the Old Testament? How could he endorse the New Testament when it wasn't written yet?

Do you agree with Dr. Kenneth Kantzer when he says, "The Christian doesn't necessarily insist that one must believe *everything* in the Bible before He is convinced of *anything* in it"?

Why do some Christians fall into the trap of sounding as though they trust in the Bible for their salvation? What is the best way to avoid this trap?

The Supernatural point of view . . .

Colossians 2:1-3 says God's secret plan, now at last made known, is Christ Himself and that in Christ lie hidden all the untapped treasures of wisdom and knowledge. What did Christ have to say about the Scriptures? See Matt. 5:17,18; Matt. 26:53,54; Luke 18:31 and John 10:35. Write out a brief summary of His views.

Compare Col. 2:1-3 with Eph. 3:1-19. What evidence does Paul give that God communicated His plan by divine revelation (see especially Eph. 3:5). Compare II Tim. 3:16 and II Pet. 3:15,16 with Paul's statements in Eph. 3:5-7. Why are both Paul and Peter so confident of their position?

If you'd like to do some further reading . . .

Christ the Controversialist, John R. Stott, Inter-Varsity Press, 1970. See especially chapter 2, "Authority: Tradition or Scripture?" and chapter 3, "Scripture: End or Means?"

Miracles, C. S. Lewis, Macmillan, 1964, chapter 10, "Horrid Red Things" deals candidly and concisely with the metaphors of Scripture and their literal meaning.

Know Why You Believe, Paul Little, Inter-Varsity Press, 1968. See chapter 5, "Is the Bible God's Word?"

The New Testament Documents: Are They Reliable? F. F. Bruce, Inter-Varsity Press, 1960. See especially chapter 2, "The New Testament's Attestation," in which Dr. Bruce points out "There is much more evidence for the New Testament than for other ancient writings of comparable date" such as Caesar's *Gallic War* or the *Histories* of the Roman historian, Tacitus.

Can I Trust the Bible?, Moody Press, 1973. See especially chapter 1, "How May I Know the Bible Is Inspired?" by Gordon H. Clark, and chapter 9, "Is the New Testament Historically Accurate?" by Robert H. Mounce.

Quotes worth considering . . .

"An accumulation of Bible knowledge is one thing; a growing personal knowledge of Jesus Christ, whom to know is eternal life, is quite another.

"No, what is required is that we obey the Bible. The best way to honor this book as God's book is to do what it says. And if we do what it says we shall keep coming to Christ for the supply of all our needs." —John R. W. Stott[8]

Don't just sit there . . .

Think this one through: "If I had time to give only two reasons for believing the Bible is a Supernatural book, God's inspired Word, what reasons would I give?"

Write down the name of the non-Christian friend with whom you would like to share your views of God and the Bible. Pray regularly that God will help you find the opportunity to talk with this person and when the opportunity comes, take it.

CHAPTER 5

SHOULDN'T A CHRISTIAN KEEP AN OPEN·MIND?

I guess you could say I'm typical ... raised in a Christian home, went to church all my life, was in the youth group ... the whole bit.

I'm twenty years old, photographer for my school paper, and lean to the left politically. I smoke grass and hash but stay away from the hard drugs. I like to relax with wine and beer—whatever's cool.

I'm engaged. We plan to be married someday but sleep together now. I believe that love is more important than sex— that love comes first. Morality changes and it has to be a personal thing.

The way I see it, Christ isn't the only way to God. I just can't believe anymore that accepting Christ is the deciding factor in salvation. Living a good life and believing in God is the important thing.

The doctrine of the Trinity is okay—God and Christ as One. But if someone doesn't believe in Christ, that's okay too. Whatever he believes in, is another form of God—a personal

God. No matter what I do, it's all right if I think it's okay. Then God understands.

The Bible isn't divine revelation. The truth is what I have. If there is something after death (and I believe there is) then I will be saved, but I don't believe there's a hell and feelings of guilt and judgment.

I'm opposed to Christians as evangelical conservative Bible thumpers. The hell-fire approach doesn't appeal. I don't see fundamentalists talking much about a loving God. All they talk about is how evil we all are, but I don't believe in original sin. We need to be saved because we are imperfect, but not because of anything some imaginary guy named Adam did.

The above "stream-of-consciousness" is by an anonymous but very real university coed. Challenge her logic and consistency if you want to, but take note of at least two significant comments:

"The truth is what I have."

"No matter what I do, it's all right if I think it's okay. Then God understands."

In the world of the late twentieth century it is extremely popular to be open-minded. If you sound a little inconsistent and irrational it doesn't matter. "Whatever's cool" is what counts. The truth is what you have and what you have is just as good as what anybody else has.

Dogma is out. Relative thinking is in. Hard and fast answers are out and a spirit of "let's keep looking and wait and see" is in. Biblical Christianity is identified with the establishment, the rule makers who stifle true thought and open-mindedness.

The Christian in the secular crowd at the university, in the military, or on the job, often gets labeled as narrow-minded, bound by rules and traditions. Sometimes the Christian can't help but wonder if the secular peer group is right about his "narrow-mindedness." After all, when you are committed to Christ you can't go around saying, "Whatever's cool" . . . or can you? As a Christian isn't your mind "closed" at certain points? Aren't there some basic things on which a Christian must make a stand?

Since we are using Paul's letters to the Colossians to learn how to be Christians in an unchristian world, it should be useful to get his opinion on "being open-minded." Reared a Hebrew of the Hebrews, a student of the great Jewish rabbi, Gamaliel, Paul knew his theology and his philosophy. This is precisely why he fought so bitterly against Christianity at first.

As Saul,* the Jewish scholar and teacher, he thought Christianity was some sort of pagan polytheistic cult that threatened the central Jewish teaching of one God. It took a personal visit by Christ Himself in a blinding vision on the road to Damascus to turn Paul around and reveal to him that his Jewish concept of God was too small.

Paul learned that while he had been hunting Christ's followers, Christ had been hunting *him*. Paul's burning desire to love and please God was satisfied when he met Christ. The great burdens of guilt that Paul carried along with his rules and Jewish laws were rolled away. Paul knew that now he had The Answer and all the other answers were either wrong or only tiny parts of the real answer, Jesus Christ.

Paul knew that the minute Christianity started spreading its authoritative Good News, it would be challenged by those who had other ideas and viewpoints on life. Sure enough, that's exactly what happened. A strange mixture of Gnostic philosophy plus Jewish ascetics and legalism threatened to undermine the infant Christian church. This attack on Christiani-

*Paul's Jewish name before his conversion to Christ.

ty's claim to absolute and final truth in Christ was a major reason Paul wrote his letter to the Colossians and later his letter to the Ephesians.

So if you had asked Paul, "Shouldn't a Christian be open-minded?" he would have probably agreed, but with a note of caution.

"I am saying this because I am afraid that someone may fool you with smooth talk. For though I am far away from you my heart is with you, happy because you are getting along so well, happy because of your strong faith in Christ. And now just as you trusted Christ to save you, trust Him, too, for each day's problems; live in vital union with Him. Let your roots grow down into Him and draw up nourishment from Him. See that you go on growing in the Lord, and become strong and vigorous in the truth. . . . Let your lives overflow with joy and thanksgiving for all He has done"[b] (Col. 2:4-7).

Why is Paul so afraid of "smooth talk"? Is he anti-intellectual? Is he afraid that his faith can't stand up in a religious discussion?

It helps to keep in mind that in his letter to the Colossians Paul is responding to the news that heresy is on the loose in Colosse. False teachers were holding their own private little "Bible" studies in which they would imply or directly claim that Christ is not the only answer.

For the Gnostic philosophers and Jewish legalists, it was just too simple to say that Jesus Christ was sufficient for all things. They didn't want to see Jesus as someone truly unique.

To sum it up, the false teachers at Colosse were trying to convince the Christians that believing in Jesus Christ was not sufficient for salvation.[1]

But Paul isn't fooled by this kind of smooth talk and he doesn't want the Colossian Christians fooled either.

Paul knew that, like himself, the Colossian believers had been ransomed, redeemed—liberated from sin. This just wasn't so much religious jargon and cliché-tossing for Paul. As he said in Col. 1:13, Christ had actually rescued him and all Christians from the darkness and gloom of Satan's kingdom. Christ had brought all of them into His own kingdom of light. If they made the mistake of buying the false teachings (which sounded good but which were based more on philosophy and human wisdom than they were on the Gospel), the Colossians would be enslaving themsleves once more to a life of human effort. They would once again enter into the endless struggle to achieve salvation through works and mental gymnastics.

Paul uses a simple analogy to put the Colossians on the right track: They are to go on living in Christ as plants live in rich soil. Paul knew that Christ is more than another religion or another theory. *He is the very source of life itself.* If the Christian tries to "transplant himself" into other systems and viewpoints, his faith will wither and die.

Go back to Col. 1:17 and Paul's words about Christ being before all else began and His power holding everything together. It isn't a case of Paul saying: "My philosophy or my religion is the best and all other philosophies and religions are bad, worthless or second-rate." Paul is actually saying that in Christ he is in touch with final infinite truth and power. This automatically supercedes any human philosophical system ever devised or which ever could be devised.

But that isn't the way the modern mind sees it, and to learn why you have to go back over 500 years to the beginning of "modern times"—the Renaissance. Beginning in the thirteenth century, the Renaissance brought Europe out of the Dark Ages into a "golden age" of new appreciation for the arts, literature and education.

It also marked the beginning of modern natural science.

God didn't die, He got de-emphasized

Unfortunately, however, the Renaissance put more emphasis on man and his ideas and less emphasis on God. The result was that many philosophical schools and viewpoints that emerged between the Renaissance and the present time became philosophical step-children of Naturalism. In other words, Naturalism claimed them more or less by default. Some of these philosophies are the following:

Rationalism says man can figure things out for himself.

Empiricism claims that man has no valid knowledge except what he has derived from his own experience—through his senses.

Pragmatism claims that truth is what works, what guides man successfully. In other words, is it useful? Does it bring satisfaction?

Utilitarianism claims that truth is what produces the greatest happiness for the greatest number of people.

Hedonism unabashedly claims that pleasure is the chief good in life.

Idealism, as developed by German philosopher Georg Hegel, teaches that there are no absolutes. There is no longer the true (thesis) vs. the false (antithesis). Instead the true and the false have a relationship that can be found in synthesis.

Evolutionism uses Darwin's theory of natural selection (man is the result of millions of years of developing from primitive life forms) to imply that man was not created by God in His image and is therefore responsible only to himself and his own standards of behavior.

In 19th century America, philosophers like Charles Sanders Pierce and William James developed views that came to be known as pragmatism. From their work came the slogans, "All truth is relative." "Truth is what works." "The true is the expedient." They were followed by the famous progressive educator, John Dewey, whose pragmatist theories in teaching and learning deeply affected American schools in the first half of the 20th century. Dewey's influence is still felt today from kindergarten to the university level.

Humanism says that man has unlimited potential and with enough time and education he can solve all his problems.

Existentialism says life is meaningless and absurd so "do your own thing"—just be sure you are sincere and willing to take responsiblity for your choices.

Mr. Average Person has little use for philosophy, and would not consider himself a follower of any particular view. What is absolutely essential to realize, however, is that the thinking of the average person has been programmed, shaped and conditioned by all of these "isms" in one way or another. The story of modern philosophical thought is the record of how man has shifted in his ideas about truth, which he sees as no longer absolute, but relative (see cartoons above).

For example, rationalism, empiricism and pragma-

HERE'S TO NO MORE ABSOLUTES!

In Europe the idea of "no absolutes," sprang from the work of nineteenth century German philosopher Georg Hegel. Evangelical theologian Francis Schaeffer, founder of a Christian retreat at L'Abri, Switzerland, says that up until Hegel's time men thought in terms of thesis and antithesis. If something was true **(thesis)** its opposite was false **(antithesis)**. Hegel changed all that by adding what he called **synthesis**. Schaeffer pictures Hegel discussing philosophy with a friend in the local tavern, and suddenly he gets this new idea. From now on he'll not think in terms of thesis-antithesis, a horizontal cause and effect relationship. There is thesis, yes, and its opposite is antithesis, **but the answer to their relationship is always synthesis.** Schaeffer feels that the concept of "no absolutes" has caused the shift in thinking that is tremendous. He believes that historic Christianity is based on the principle of thesis-antithesis, (right versus wrong) but Hegel's views on synthesis have caused a shift that dilutes and robs Christianity of its meaning.

tism are all a part of today's educational picture. Secular educators pride themselves on urging each student to, "Think for yourself. Go to the sources, experiment. Get the facts, not opinions."

Now, "thinking for yourself" is not necessarily all bad. A lot of Christians could do a lot more of it. And Christians should admit that there's nothing wrong with going to the sources and experimenting and getting facts, not just opinions.

But there's a catch. Typically speaking, views such as rationalism, empiricism or pragmatism seem to fit more comfortably in the Naturalist's chair. As you think for yourself and trust only what your senses can measure, it is only natural to start neglecting the Supernatural and then to rule out the Bible and Christ completely.

Sadly enough, a great deal of philosophical inquiry all through history has been made by people who were reacting badly to religious church machinery, which had encrusted the Gospel of Christ in rules, regulations and the overall grip of the so-called Establishment or System. Many a philosopher was reacting against the religious system (the bath water) and he threw out Jesus Christ (the Baby) at the same time.

Unfortunately, modern society—to a great degree—does the same thing, and all in the name of human progress and enlightenment. Today's student is trained practically from the cradle to be suspicious of religion and any system that claims absolute truth. This isn't necessarily a direct secular assault on the church. It's just that secular society works from different presuppositions. And the chief presupposition is that the Supernatural isn't really there.

If you must have religion, say the secularists, you must at least garb it in respectable terms that fit in with a naturalistically based world view.

Christians live in two worlds

No wonder then that many a Christian young person feels he lives in two separate worlds. What he hears from his parents and his church and his pastor is based on the authority of God's Word, the absolute truth claimed by the Bible and Jesus Christ. But at school—out in the everyday world of his peer group—it is another ball game. There is no absolute truth because all truth is relative. The truth is what works.

It may be unpleasant, but it is absolutely necessary for today's Christian, over or under thirty, to understand what all of this means. New Testament Christianity, based on the absolute truth claimed in God's revealed Word and in His personal revelation in Jesus Christ, is at complete odds with the secular modern mind.

Christ does not say, "I have some truth so why don't you try me just a little bit because I may be of some help." Christ says: "I am The Way, The Truth, and The Life because I am God, the very One who created you, the One who created this entire universe." (Review Colossians chapter 1. Also see John 14:6 and John 1:1-13.)

Jesus Christ says, "I have not come to enslave you but to give you freedom—freedom from guilt, freedom from fear of death, freedom to become everything that I know you can and want to be." (See John 10:10 and Rom. 5:2.)

The response of the modern secular mind to Christ's offer is: "Sounds like you're trying to curb my freedom. Religious dogma is not for me. I want to be open-minded, think for myself, do my own thing, sail my own seas."

What, then, does Jesus mean by "truth and freedom"? Isn't He saying that to be truly free you have to be under some kind of control? How free is a train if it is off its tracks? How free is an airliner without its navigational beam? How free is a spacecraft with no connection back to ground-control?

The world held its breath while Apollo XIII struggled back to earth after a crippling explosion. Once the spacecraft rounded the moon and headed back to earth, one of the main worries was that the damaged ship would somehow miss the "slot" where it had to enter earth's atmosphere and it would come in at too high or too low an angle and skip off into space. If that had happened, the astronauts would have been beyond

I THINK FOR MYSELF...
I GET THE FACTS... I
EXPERIMENT... I'M
OPEN-MINDED!

NATURALIST

TWO APPROACHES

all human help. They would have been free indeed and they would have perished in the "complete freedom" of outer space.

Oddly enough, when it comes to what life is really all about modern man seems to have cut himself adrift in a kind of spiritual-ethical outer space. He has deliberately cut himself off from God by simply saying that God does not exist or if He does exist, He does not have much to say. In fact, man writes God's script and lets Him say what man wants Him to. This is precisely what liberal theologians did when they started carving up the Bible and deciding what was true and what was false.*

In liberal or any other modern theology, the tenden-

---

*Liberalism developed right along with all of the "isms" that started popping up during the Renaissance and in following centuries. Liberalism had its heyday in the nineteenth and early twentieth centuries and has since then been replaced by neoorthodoxy and various forms of modernism such as the "God is dead" fad.

GOD IS MY CREATOR. CHRIST IS MY LORD. ALL TRUTH IS OPEN TO ME AND I AM OPEN TO ALL TRUTH.

SUPERNATURALIST

TO OPEN-MINDEDNESS

cy is to place more emphasis on what man says or experiences and less emphasis on what God has supposedly revealed to man in the Bible. But the trouble with that kind of God—one with nothing really authoritative to say—is that *He is not really God.* He is a sort of idol. Perhaps the greatest tragedy of modern times is that so many have made Jesus into an idol. He is "good old plastic Jesus"—a little figurine you can take down off the shelf and shine up now and then if you feel so inclined. Of course, if you have outgrown religion and all that superstitious stuff you don't have to shine up that little plastic statue. You can simply shine it on.

When it comes to Jesus Christ, you have three choices:

You can shine Him up. Keep Him on a shelf with all the rest of your idols and let Him speak only when it seems that it's appropriate and what He says seems to fit in with what you've already decided.

You can shine Him on. You can ignore Him as a piece of superstitious drivel from the Dark Ages, who is no longer relevant to modern man.

Or, you can tune Him in. As Paul puts it, if you can sink your roots deep into Christ and draw nourishment from Him, He can help you with each day's problems and He can help you grow as a person. (See Col. 2:6,7.)

Interestingly enough, you can do any one of these three things with Jesus and still come out of it with "an open mind." Paul knew this. That's why Paul was afraid that some people could fool Christians with their smooth talk. Paul knew that "having an open mind" is a relative term. You can fill an open mind with whatever you choose.

FROM WHERE YOU SIT

Are there certain points on which the Christian's mind is closed? Are there basic things where the Christian must make a stand and say "all truth is *not* relative"?

What kind of freedom does Christ offer you? Why do so many people refuse His offer? How do you define freedom?

Do you agree that you can fill an open mind with anything you choose? Can a Christian do this? In what way?

The Supernatural point of view . . .

Review Col. 2:4-7. Why is Paul afraid that the Colossian Christians could be fooled by smooth talk? According to these verses, what is the best insurance against being fooled into accepting counterfeit Christianity or views that aren't Christian at all?

Why can Paul be so sure that in Christ he has the best? Is Paul being bigoted and narrow-minded? Or, does he know something? Review Col. 1:15-23.

What do you think it means to "live in vital union with Christ"? Compare John 15:1-10; James 4:8; Ps. 16:8; 145:18. In all these verses, what is involved? Is Christianity a passive or an active faith?

If you'd like to do some further reading . . .

Philosophy and the Christian Faith, Colin Brown, Inter-Varsity Press, 1969. Probably the best book you can find that surveys the main thinkers and intellectual movements of the past thousand years, showing how all this affects being a Christian today.

Quotes worth considering . . .

"Edward Arlington Robinson once said, 'The world is not a prison home but a kind of spiritual kindergarten, where millions of bewildered infants are trying to spell God with the wrong blocks.' By accepting Jesus Christ into my heart through faith, I have found the right blocks."—Nancy Anthony, Wisconsin State U.[2]

Don't just sit there . . .

Get together with a Christian friend or two and discuss what it means to be a Christian and be open-minded. How open-minded do your friends think they are? At what points do they agree that the Christian's mind must be "closed"?

How do you and your friends feel about Christianity's claim to absolute truth in spiritual and moral areas? Does this limit the Christian in living effectively in a secular unchristian world?

CHAPTER 6

HOW OPEN ARE THE OPEN·MINDED?

YOU ONLY GO
AROUND ONCE
IN LIFE...

"Sure, I could take better care of myself. I suppose I could eat nothing but organic foods, get eight hours of sleep every night, stop smoking, things like that. It would add a couple of years to my life, but what the hell?"

—Remark made to newspaper interviewer by rock music superstar Janis Joplin less than a year before her death from an overdose of drugs.[1]

No, this isn't going to be a chapter on the evils of drugs and rock music. But Janis Joplin's life-style ("It's a rush,* honey"), illustrates aptly a prevailing philoso-

*Doper term for the "high" received when on drugs.

phy that is admired, imitated and lived out to various degrees in secular society today. This philosophy might be called "pop existentialism," which is society's way of taking the ideas of atheistic existentialism and boiling them down to suit the man on the street, the boys in the back room and the couples in parked cars.

Today much of the unchristian world acts as if it just doesn't care. What counts is being open-minded, making your statement, getting it on, doing your thing, and as long as nobody gets hurt, anything goes! In short, life is meaningless except for what you can make of it as the present moment. As one beer commercial put it: "You only go around once in life . . . grab all the gusto you can!"

Meanwhile, back in Col. 2:8-10, the apostle Paul is all for gusto, but he believes in getting it in another way:

"Don't let others spoil your faith and joy with their philosophies, their wrong and shallow answers built on men's thoughts and ideas, instead of on what Christ has said. For in Christ there is all of God in a human body; *so you have everything when you have Christ,* and you are filled with God through your union with Christ. He is the highest Ruler, with authority over every other power"[b] (Col. 2:8-10).

Obviously Paul would not buy the open-minded pop existentialism being peddled by today's drug pushers, movie makers, entertainers, playboys, champions of the new morality, sexual revolutionaries, porno salesmen, et al. It's not that what they're saying is just naughty, dirty or immoral. A lot of it unquestionably is, but what is basically wrong with pop existentialism is its Naturalistic foundation. The Supernatural is ruled out or not taken seriously. To be sure, a lot of people still seem to be talking about God, but the overwhelming attitude across secular society is that man is in charge and that God is an idea, a goal of some kind rather than the Creator of the universe who can be known in the Person of Jesus Christ.

The Bible teaches that in the beginning God created man. Today's modern mind has reversed the order. People like to think that man has created God and pop existentialism leads them into thinking that they can be God because they live in virtual autonomy, answering to no one but themselves and their own desires.

Ironically, modern existentialism supposedly started with Danish theologian Soren Kierkegaard. Back in the mid-nineteenth century, Kierkegaard rebelled against the deadness of the Lutheran state church in Denmark, his native land. Kierkegaard wrote in his journal, "The thing is to understand myself, and see what God really wishes me to do; the thing is to find the truth which is true for me, to find the idea for which I can live and die."[2]

Existentialism split into two streams

From Kierkegaard's emphasis on personal experience and personal opinion, two streams of existential thought emerge. One was God-centered, or at least, pseudotheological. The other extreme led to the jaded atheism of the twentieth century.[*]

For example, Jean-Paul Sartre, possibly the most famous proponent of atheistic existentialism, has written:

"Man can count on no one but himself; he is alone,

*Existentialism, like many concepts or views, has many shades of meaning. Many devout men who sincerely trust Christ would call themselves "existential" in the sense that, like Kierkegaard, they want to be deeply involved with God in a meaningful way. When built on a Supernatural foundation, which recognizes Christ as Creator and sustainer of life, existential concern can draw you closer to God. But when built on a Naturalist foundation, existentialism leads to despair, disillusionment and moral anarchy because God is left out of the picture.

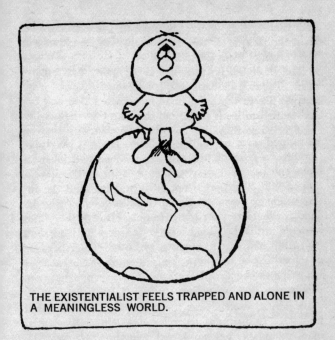

THE EXISTENTIALIST FEELS TRAPPED AND ALONE IN A MEANINGLESS WORLD.

abandoned on earth in the midst of his infinite responsibilities, without help, with no other aim than the one he sets himself, with no other destiny than the one that he forges for himself on this earth."

In his play, *No Exit*, one of Sartre's three principle characters, Garcin, says: "Wait a minute, there's a snag somewhere; something disagreeable. Why, now, should it be disagreeable? . . . I see; it's life without a break."

This is Garcin's way of recognizing the absurdity of life. The setting for the play is a windowless room from which there is no escape. He shares the room with two women and all three of them can't bear one another. Each person tries to dominate the other two but always fails. Estelle wants to kill Inez so that she can have

Garcin. Of course she can't because Inez is dead already. In fact, *everyone* in the play is dead already. Garcin finally understands that he is in hell. He says, "What? Only two of you? I thought there were more; many more. So this is hell. I'd never have believed it . . . hell is—other people!"[3]

It is with this kind of writing that Sartre paints the existential picture of life.* Existential man feels that he is trapped on a meaningless planet. He was put there through no fault of his own. He is alone and he must make the best of it. His existence is all that is important to him. The past is not even prologue and the future might not even be there. He lives for now and he chooses whatever suits him. He does his own thing and he feels justified as long as "no one gets hurt." If you try to tell him that someone may be hurt later because of something he does now, he is unimpressed because as far as he is concerned there is no connection between events, acts or happenings.

Existential man claims that he is free. He says that he is free from traditions, rules and dogma. Existential man claims he has no moral hang-ups. He says he makes up his own morals as he goes along. His main goal in life is to be, to "do his thing."

Existentialism (in its modern form at least) wasn't around when Paul wrote Col. 2:8-10, but when you read these verses against a background of twentieth century hopelessness, restlessness, meaninglessness and cynicism, which are all typical of existential despair, they take on new and potent meaning.

---

*Sartre's work is widely known, but serious scholars of existentialism see Sartre as only a small branch of a very much larger tree. William Barrett, for example, writing in his book *Irrational Man* (Doubleday Anchor Books, 1958) believes that two Germans, Martin Heidegger (1889-   ) and Karl Jaspers (1883-1969) are ". . . strictly speaking the creators of existential philosophy in this century . . ." (p. 11).

ARE SUPERNATURALISTS LEFT
HOLDING THE BAG?

Different translations of Col. 2:8-10 display vividly the bankruptcy in the motto, "Do your own thing."

From the *Jerusalem Bible*—"Make sure that no one traps you and deprives you of your freedom by some secondhand, empty, rational philosophy based on the principles of this world instead of on Christ. . . ."

From the Phillips' translation—"Be careful that nobody spoils your faith through intellectualism or high-sounding nonsense. . . ."

From the *New English Bible*—"Be on your guard; do not let your minds be captured by hollow and delusive speculations, based on traditions of man-made teaching. . . ."

Again and again, the warning is clear: don't be trapped . . . be on your guard . . . don't let others spoil your faith. . . .

This Biblical view doesn't sound too open-minded—at least in the secular sense of the word. The unchristian world prides itself on its open-mindedness, its tolerance and what it calls human understanding. Sometimes the Christian can't help wondering if he hasn't been left holding his bag of Biblical absolutes, with no place to go. So many of his friends seem to be playing it cool and loose. They seem to have no hang-ups, no laws and codes that cramp their life-style. The existentialist's battle-cry, "Do your own thing!" can sound pretty good to a person who feels that the church has been making him do its thing all of his life and he's never really been free.

David grew up like a good Christian should

That was what happened to David Knighton, son of a prominent Christian leader, Dr. J. Raymond Knighton, president of Medical Assistance Programs, an organization that channels drugs and hospital supplies and equipment to Christian missionaries throughout the world. David grew up like a good Christian boy should, always attending church and Sunday School, getting good grades and never causing any trouble. David seemed to accept what his church impressed upon him—a Christianity that was a religion of rules. The church told him how to dress, how to act, how to think.

In relating his experience in *Decision* magazine David points out that perhaps the church leaders didn't want to give this rule-bound impression but he feels it was inevitable. They had been brought up the same way and that's the way things were.

David went over a lot of Bible stories but seldom

80

saw any relationship between these stories and real life. Ethics, personal behavior, the why's and wherefore's of personal conduct, were not discussed. If he asked why he should bother to study the stories, he was given an obscure answer that reflected an attitude of "accept what we say as *the* right way."

David went into junior high and not only did this mean a new school but it also meant a new neighborhood and a new church. For the first time his pat rules didn't fit. Even some of the junior high students he went to church with didn't always obey those rules. While David remained on the side of the rule makers, he was fighting a civil war inside. His friends said they were Christians, but they had the same life-style and values as non-Christians at school. It looked to David as if they were having all the fun while he held on to his bag of Christian laws which said no dancing, no wild parties, etc.

Then came high school and David decided to try the "jet set" in his sophomore year. He went to parties and hobnobbed with the athletes but that turned out to be as dissatisfying as the shallow rule-centered Christianity he had been trying to practice. So David wound up in a sort of no man's land between a legalistic Christianity and the secular life-style typical in high school today.

During his junior year in high school he took a course in advanced French and had to read Albert Camus' *The Stranger*. The story told of a young man who searched for the meaning of life. He tried everything, even religion, but his existence seemed useless and insignificant. Finally, as he faced the guillotine for an unpardonable crime, the man decided that death is the only reasonable answer to existence. David's reaction to this story could have been increased pessimism and hopelessness with his own plight, but instead an interesting thing happened. He says:

"Camus forced me to recognize that the life of legalistic Christianity I was living was preposterous because it didn't work. In other words, he showed me what I was going through. That forced me back to the Bible. I had been reading the Bible once in a while but not regularly at all. Now I was being thrown into a search to find out what kind of meaning Jesus gave to life, if any. And as I read the Gospels, they appeared to me in a new light. The Bible was no longer just a book. I went beyond Camus' point of absurdity and found that Jesus Christ was the only lasting answer; that it was he who gave meaning to life. It all sort of fell into place."[4]

An atheist led him to Christ

And so through the writings of Albert Camus—atheist and existentialist who saw no reasonable answer for human existence—David Knighton came to a real and living faith in Jesus Christ! A little later, David's French instructor asked the class what they thought of existentialist concepts.

David answered by recalling that Jean-Paul Sartre said that when man finally realizes life is totally absurd he has one of two alternatives: He can choose death or he can take on a meaningful project. David commented that he didn't think that either alternative made a lot of sense. And then he told the class of the third alternative that he had chosen—totally committing himself in a personal relationship with the only perfect Man, Jesus Christ. He told the class that this relationship, this friendship with the God-man Jesus Christ, had given a new and exciting purpose to his life.

It was the first public testimony David had ever given, and he gave it in a French class in the French language! He was startled, not with testifying for Christ in French, but because what he said made so much sense. It changed his whole outlook on life. During his senior year in high school, Christianity was a live issue, not a dead thing. It was something he could talk about and get excited about. As he says:

"Before I hadn't really been able to give a rational answer when somebody asked me about being a Christian. I know it's a matter of faith but when I talked to my friends I had to speak from a reasonable standpoint, and now I had one. Furthermore, I no longer have to worry about a superficial code of conduct. That crutch isn't needed to make Christianity viable. I enjoy a beautiful day-by-day relationship with the One who made me and am involved in the task of communicating the reality of existence through Christ."[5]

What David Knighton discovered was that the open-mindedness of a secular existentialistic life-style is not open-mindedness at all. In fact, it shut him off from real freedom of thought which has to include the Supernaturalist as well as the Naturalist point of view. At the same time he found release from what he knew was not open-mindedness—a religious legalism, a Christianity made of plastic handcuffs, strong enough to be binding and inhibiting, but too weak to really hold you.

David Knighton found that only one thing can really hold you—cords of love for the Supreme Person, Jesus Christ. And he found that these cords of love aren't made solely of emotion and good feeling. There is also a reason, the assurance that what you have is real, that it makes sense.

All this is precisely why Paul writes to the Colossians with warnings against heresy and vain philosophies. Paul doesn't suffer from philosophical paranoia. It's just that he knows that when you have the best you should not settle for anything less. If you start with the best—Jesus Christ—then you have Everything. You are filled with God through your union with Him (Col. 2:10).

Actually then, as the Christian operates within the Supernaturalist context he can be as open-minded as he wants, because he has a valid standard for truth. When you're properly connected to the One who created you, you are free to take the good ideas from all viewpoints —including existentialism. Put Christ in His proper place—as Lord of your life—and you will have the wisdom and discernment to sort things out no matter how bewildering and complex they get. If you know Christ as He wants to know you, you are free indeed. You can be open to all that is good in life, all that God offers. Then you grow and change according to God's program, not your own.

The so-called open-mindedness of those who sit in the Naturalist's chair always beckons, trying to lure you away from Christ. And on the other side, you face the danger of slipping into legalism, rules and codes, and cultural hang-ups of all kinds. But for some reason—it has something to do with His great love for us—Christ doesn't bind us to Him with cords so tight that we can't move in any direction. He allows us to be free to make our choice and ironically enough, freedom to make choices is exactly what the existentialists say they want.

God loves us enough to give us freedom to stray if we want to. God pays every Christian the ultimate compliment of allowing him to be a pure existentialist —who makes his choices as a responsible person, but realizing that he is made in the image of the Supreme Person, Jesus Christ. The Christian doesn't choose in a world that is empty, meaningless and a cruel joke. The Christian knows that life is a lot more than a room with no exit in a hell made of other people.

The Christian knows that secular open-mindedness is really secular emptiness, but Christian open-mindedness leads to spiritual fullness. As Paul says: You have

everything when you have Christ and you are filled
with God through your union with Him!

FROM WHERE YOU SIT

What is your definition of open-mindedness? Why do
the pop-existentialists think they are open-minded? Is
the Christian more or less open-minded? Why?

What is the difference between secular (Naturalist)
open-mindedness and Christian (Supernatural) open-
mindedness? Is the difference crucial for you? Why?

The Supernatural point of view . . .

What does Paul mean when he uses the term, "vain
philosophies" in Col. 2:8? Does he mean that all philosophical thought is a waste of time? At what point does
philosophy become vain as far as Paul is concerned?
What clues do you find in Col. 2:9,10?

Compare Col. 2:8-10 with other warnings that Paul
issued to early Christians: I Tim. 1:7 (false teachers); 4:2; 6:3; II Tim. 4:3; Titus 1:11. Also see Peter's
warnings about apostasy and heresy—II Pet. 2:1—actually the entire second chapter of II Peter, which goes
into great detail on "marks of false teachers." Also see
Jesus' words of warning in Matt. 16:6.

Jesus, Paul and Peter continually warn against false
teaching, false doctrine. Why do they feel this is so important? In the final analysis what is more important:
right beliefs or right actions? Read Col. 2:8-10 carefully
before you commit yourself.

If you want to read further . . .

What Is Human? T. M. Kitwood, Inter-Varsity Press,
1970, a brief paperback of 137 pages which analyzes

humanism and existentialism and compares these two views to Christianity.

Irrational Man, William Barrett, Doubleday Anchor Books, 1958. A thorough survey of existentialism by a secular scholar which is called, "The finest definition of existentialism ever written." If you are serious in wanting to know more about existentialism, this 314-page paperback is a good place to start.

"Existentialism: A Net to Catch a Fog," article by Vernon C. Grounds, *Eternity,* August 1971, make good points on the difficulty in defining and describing existentialism, and at the same time discusses some of its major concepts.

Quotes worth considering . . .

"Lying deep-rooted in our human nature is a basic objection to Christianity. 'I don't want to live under God's control,' we say. 'I want to run my own life in freedom and independence. Even if I do make a mess of it, at least it will be by my own effort. I'm free. And becoming a slave doesn't appeal to me at all.'

"But Jesus Christ says: 'On the contrary, you *are* a slave. I have come so that you can become free.' "
—Robert Crossley, *We Want to Live*[6]

Don't just sit there

Take inventory. Is your life-style determined by the "rules of your faith" (your Christian code of conduct) or by your relationship to Christ? Or, is it hard to tell the difference between the two? Talk this over first with a Christian friend. And then try it with a non-Christian friend. See if you can communicate to your non-Christian friend why you "don't do certain things," and why you participate in a lot of what he probably thinks are "religious activities."

Create *YOUR* Christian Life-Style

For six chapters you've been looking over the secular scene, trying to get a picture of how the unchristian world thinks and why Christ is the only answer to its hopelessness, meaninglessness and pessimism.

Now it's time to talk about developing a Christian life-style that works for you, makes you effective.

But that means wrestling with some tough questions:

Is my Christian life-style legalistic or based on love?

Does my life-style reveal a relationship with Christ or a walk with a rule book?

Does my life-style help me be fair, honest, kind, considerate or are my ethics an ego trip?

Does my life-style include real Christian community (fellowship) or am I a Lone Ranger Christian?

Does my life-style help me reach out with the Gospel or lash out with my religion?

Do I have (or even want) a Christian life-style, when it's much easier to live in No Sweat City, cooperating with the secular cookie-cutter, getting all the goodies I can?

You can have a Christian life-style that is effective, fun and successful. The possibilities are unlimited. As Paul says, "You are living a brand new kind of life that is continually learning more and more of what is right, and trying constantly to be more and more like Christ who created this new life within you"[b] (Col. 3:10).

CHAPTER 7

HOW (NOT) TO PLAY

WISH I WERE A BETTER CHRISTIAN!

Developing a Christian life-style starts with getting your head straight about just how things really are between God and you.

There's no point in playing little games to convince everyone (including yourself) that you are spiritual. Too many Christians have always done that. There's even a book out on it: *Games Christians Play.*[1] It's a funny book, but it's sad, too, because it so accurately exposes typical legalistic codes and hypocritical hangups.

Inspiration for *Games Christians Play* was undoubtedly psychiatrist Eric Berne's book, *Games People Play.* According to Dr. Berne, most of us go through life faking it, or wearing a mask, a great deal of the time. Because being real, open and honest is too frightening, we play "games." Among Berne's classifications are life games, marital games, party games, sexual games—all are ". . . substitutes for the real living of real intimacy."

For example, a typical party game is WHY DON'T YOU—YES, BUT. To play, you make a complaint about a friend, a teacher, an employer, your spouse . . . whoever. Several other people in the group give you suggestions on what to do about it, but each time you say, "Yes, but . . ." and then you shoot down that suggestion with several reasons why it won't work for you. (You have, of course, thought all this out well beforehand and really don't want any help. You just want to play games.) WDY—YB finally ends with you the winner, when nobody else can think of any more solutions for your vexing problem.[3]

Berne claims that all of us are taught to play games from infancy, that "Raising children is primarily a matter of teaching them what games to play."[4]

All of this has its parallels to the Christian life. As a person grows up in the church (or comes into a church at any point in life), he is taught to play the Christian games that are favorites in that particular religious environment. It all adds up to what might be called the biggest Christian game of all: WISH I WERE A BETTER CHRISTIAN.

In WIWABC, Christ is not so much a companion or friend (or even a Saviour) as He is "The Master Coach" —ever present with stopwatch, always urging you to better your own time, jump a little higher, or throw a little farther. For the player of WIWABC, the Bible is the rule book and Christian education is basically a process of "learning the rules." And if anything can take the style out of Christian living it's the rumble with the rules, the constant gnawing in your gut because you are not living up to what you think you are supposed to do and be.

Nobody experienced this with more intensity than Paul. Nobody lived by the rule book more carefully. A Pharisee of the Pharisees, that was Paul. He had been the class of his field. He knew the rule book* backward, forward and upside down. And he had obeyed those rules to the last dot on the *i* and the last cross on the *t*.

And then Paul met Christ.

Did Paul just chuck all the rules and live as he pleased? No, he simply found out that rules are a *means, not an end.* As he wrote to one church, "The Jewish laws were our teacher and guide until Christ came to give us right standing with God through our faith" (Gal. 3:24).

The reason Christ turned Paul's life inside out was that Christ did something for him that the rule book and playing legalistic games never did. Christ gave him peace, freedom from guilt. Before Christ, Paul's religion had been strictly in his head. But his stomach had been a bonfire of frustration, with the awareness that he was just not making it.

That's why Paul minced no words when he heard about the Gnostic brand of WIWABC at Colosse:

"So don't let anyone criticize you for what you eat or drink, or for not celebrating Jewish holidays and feasts or new moon ceremonies or Sabbaths. For these were only temporary rules that ended when Christ came. They were only shadows of the real thing—of Christ Himself.

"Don't let anyone declare you lost when you refuse to worship angels, as they say you must. They have seen a vision, they say, and know you should. These proud men . . . have a very clever imagination. But they are not connected to Christ, the Head to which all of us who are His body are joined; for we are joined together by His strong sinews and we grow only as we get our nourishment and strength from God.

*The Pharisees' "rule book" was the Torah, which not only included the Old Testament Scriptures but the whole body of religious literature of Judaism inherited from prophets, priests and wise men.

"Since you died, as it were, with Christ and this has set you free from following the world's ideas of how to be saved—by doing good and obeying various rules—why do you keep right on following them anyway, still bound by such rules as not eating, tasting, or even touching certain foods? Such rules are mere human teachings, for food was made to be eaten and used up. These rules may seem good, for rules of this kind require strong devotion and are humiliating and hard on the body, but they have no effect when it comes to conquering a person's evil thoughts and desires. They only make him proud"^b (Col. 2:16-23).

What Paul is talking about here are the games that the Gnostic phonies were teaching the Colossian Christians. Being good game players they put heavy emphasis on ascetics—strict discipline, rigid training. They emphasized the idea that the body is evil and only the spirit is good.

The Gnostics were training the Colossian Christians in the art of the "no-no" by telling them what they could eat or drink—take into their bodies. They were also telling them how they should spend their time, what days were really important, which feasts to attend.

This all has a familiar ring. The art of the "no-no" is still important for playing today's brand of WISH I WERE A BETTER CHRISTIAN and its many derivatives. For example, there is that favorite game, GOOD CHRISTIANS DON'T . . . (drink, smoke, dance, go to movies, or do "other worldly things"—depending on the cultural emphasis in your particular environment).*

Another popular pastime is GET ON THE BALL (and shape up—"like the Bible says you should").

*This is not to say that Christians *should* drink, smoke, etc. For some ideas on selecting the programming for *your* computer, see chapters 8, 9.

WIWABC COMES IN VARIOUS PACKAGES.

GOTB is a good game for those feeling guilty about needing to "please God more." Players of this game tend to see God primarily as THE JUDGE—the One who is keeping count in much the same way judges score figure-skating, gymnastics or high-diving: ten possible points is perfect, followed by nine, eight, seven, six, etc., depending on how imperfectly you perform.

GET ON THE BALL is easy to play in regard to your devotional life (Bible reading, prayer) or your discipleship (witnessing, serving in the church). It is a favorite sermon topic. Most congregations hear a GOTB sermon every few months, some, every few weeks.

Paul has only one thing to say about the art of the "no-no", playing Christian games and all the various rules and codes that go along with it. Why drift away from Christ, and, ironically enough, go back to the *world's* ideas of how to be saved—by doing good deeds, obeying various rules, slavishly following certain systems and rituals?

So how do you go beyond games? How do you escape the tentacles of legalism without backsliding into spiritual apathy, drunk on the wine of "cheap grace"?

Following are six positive specific things you can do to identify causes of legalism in your life and get rid of them. If you'd like, make it a dialog with your alter ego and ask yourself these questions:

1. *Have I experienced the difference between going through religious motions and living with the Real Thing?*

This is exactly what Paul is getting at back in Col. 2:11,12, when he says: "When you came to Christ He set you free from your evil desires, not by a bodily operation of circumcision but by a spiritual operation, the baptism of your souls. For in baptism you see how your old, evil nature died with Him and was buried with Him; and then you came up out of death with Him into a new life because you trusted the Word of the mighty God who raised Christ from the dead."[b]

Paul had firsthand experience with going through outward religious motions instead of allowing God to inwardly change and motivate him. Like many religious rituals the rite of Jewish circumcision had simply become a duty, a "badge" that signified membership in the Jewish religious club.[*]

Paul knew that any priest could circumcise—remove the foreskin from a man's body—but only Jesus Christ

---

*Circumcision was instituted by God when He made His covenant with Abraham (Gen. 17:10). Originally, it had deep significance and was an outward sign of inward commitment and devotion to God. But as the centuries passed, more and more Jews saw it as something they did out of habit and tradition. It had no meaning for them, except to give them the assurance that if a person was circumcised he was completely right with God. The parallel with today's trust in religious activities instead of in God is tragically obvious.

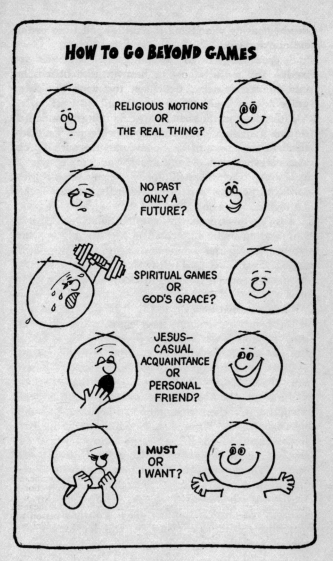

HOW TO GO BEYOND GAMES

RELIGIOUS MOTIONS
OR
THE REAL THING?

NO PAST
ONLY A
FUTURE?

SPIRITUAL GAMES
OR
GOD'S GRACE?

JESUS—
CASUAL
ACQUAINTANCE
OR
PERSONAL
FRIEND?

I MUST
OR
I WANT?

could cut away everything that keeps you from loving and obeying God. That's why Paul talks about a "spiritual operation," or a "circumcision made without hands." When the Christian believer is baptized, he goes through an act of obedience to Christ, signifying his identification with Christ's death and resurrection.

With any operation there must be cutting and that includes a spiritual operation. The keen edge of repentance must be part of any conversion because this is what cuts away the old life which was completely sold out to sin. Unfortunately today repentance is often looked on as some sort of superspiritual, corny cliché. But repentance is not corny and it is no cliché. Repentance is "an inward change of mind, affections, convictions, and commitment, rooted in the fear of God and sorrow for offenses committed against Him, which, when accompanied by faith in Jesus Christ, results in an outward turning from sin to God and His service in all of life."[5]

When a person believes in Christ he doesn't just take all the benefits—salvation, forgiveness, peace of mind, "cool" feelings. There's a lot more to believing in Christ than just joining a church or grooving with some inner circle of beautiful people who think Jesus is a soul man. There is more to believing in Christ than checking off the steps in conversion and inviting God to be your cosmic buddy. There is supposed to be inward change and commitment. There should be real sorrow for past offenses against God. If there is no sorrow for offenses, how can reconciliation take place? To be reconciled means, "Things are okay again between you and the other person." In this case, the other person is God. *But the one who has to change is you.* You are the one who was not okay in the first place. You have to turn from what was not okay (your sin) and decide to go the other way—God's Way.

2. Do I really believe that in Christ I don't have a past—only a future?

It's strange how a lot of us keep thinking the Gospel is too good to be true. Some of us don't see our introduction to Christ the way Paul did: *a total new start as a person* . . .

"You were dead in your sins, and your sinful desires were not yet cut away. Then He gave you a share in the very life of Christ, for He forgave all your sins, and blotted out the charges proved against you, the list of His commandments which you had not obeyed. He took this list of sins and destroyed it by nailing it to Christ's cross. In this way God took away Satan's power to accuse you of sin, and God openly displayed to the whole world Christ's triumph at the cross where your sins were all taken away"[b] (Col. 2:13-15).

It's comforting to know the Scriptural teaching that our sins are nailed to Christ's cross and the charges against us are literally blotted out. But deep inside, it's possible to wonder if God's sense of justice wasn't short-circuited—at least a little bit.

Paul is saying that before you knew Christ, you were on death row—dead in your sins. Christ comes into your life and for some strange reason you go free. What Jesus did wiped out all charges against you.

It's like signing a confession for murder and then having the judge burn it. It's even better than that. You are pardoned completely for your crimes. You walk out of death row, the prison of self, a completely free person. At least in God's sight you're free. But it's up to you to really believe Satan is defeated, that Christ is number one, that you are on the winning side —forever.

As a Christian you never look back. You concentrate on the future and becoming what God wants you to be.

3. *Do I know how to avoid being trapped into playing spiritual games?*

In his book, *Sinners Anonymous,* H. S. Vigeveno observes, "It is strange that with all our emphasis on the Grace of God (which means God's free love toward men who never merit such love) we place demands upon Christians to shape up and do those things which are required in the Bible."[6]

In a chapter discussing legalism, Vigeveno talks about the traps in making such decisions as keeping up with your devotions (no Bible, no breakfast) or committing yourself to witnessing to one person a day.

Vigeveno wonders: "Why do we never hear . . . that we are not able to keep any of our decisions? It is not within our power, no matter how eagerly we may try to live the Christian life successfully. We are not self-sufficient. We have gradually moved out of the realm of Grace—which means we have entered the field of works: 'We can keep our own decisions, if only we make the right ones.' No, we cannot. Not even Christian decisions. We are always dependent on God. The more we make and break decisions, the worse guilt feelings we incur. Christianity is not a legalistic carrying out of Christian duties, but it should become a daily, personal relationship with our Heavenly Father."[7]

Is Vigeveno saying that Christians should not try to have devotions regularly, that they shouldn't try to witness or keep themselves separate from the secular value system? No, but he is saying there is a subtle difference between legalism and faith.

Works (legalism) is trusting your own efforts.

Faith is trusting in Christ—*depending* on God Himself.

Trouble is, this difference is so simple, so ordinary, that a lot of us write it off because we have "heard all that before." And so we go on playing our games, trying very hard to be spiritual, to please God, and having an extremely difficult time living as Christians in an unchristian world.

The reason it is difficult is because playing games is a life of legalism. So, no matter how fervently you testify on the outside about trusting Christ, on the inside a little red neon sign spells out G-U-I-L-T. Psychiatrist Eric Berne points out that games have an ulterior quality. Players are always looking for a payoff. "Every game . . . is basically dishonest. . . ."[8]

No wonder then that you feel guilt. You are being dishonest with others, with yourself and (obviously) with God. But there's a way to turn off the guilt. In matters of interpersonal relationships, Eric Berne says you can rise above the programming of the past to the spontaneous game-free candidness of an aware person. You can experience "something that is more rewarding than games and that is intimacy."[9] In matters spiritual, you can do the same thing, and that brings us to the next very practical question . . .

4. *Do I know Jesus personally or casually?*

A warm friendship can never ripen if one person ignores the other or "only sees him occasionally." When you want to become intimate friends with someone you spend time with that person. You really get to know that person and let that person know you. And when you really know someone, you open yourselves to one another. There is a trust, a feeling of oneness between you.

Intimacy—oneness with you—is just what Jesus is interested in. "Take care to live in Me," He told his disciples the night before the cross, "and let Me live in you . . ."[b] (John 15:4).

For some reason, this isn't easy. Even with Jesus it is

99

hard to trust, to be open and honest. Eric Berne says moving beyond games is frightening to many people so they stick with their games. Could it be we prefer legalism and Christian games rather than intimacy with Christ and the brethren?

But suppose you say you want to try going beyond games, that you want to create a Christian life-style that is game-free? This will be difficult, particularly if you have been taught and preached to all your life about being a better Christian and getting on the ball for Jesus. The way to start is not to worry about "getting on the ball" for Jesus but simply start sharing your life with Him.

Now admittedly there is a catch. If you really want to know what Jesus has to tell you—in *any* situation—you have to be spending time with Him and that means prayer and reading His written Word. Then, when the sticky situation (or any situation) comes up, Christ is right there with you. In fact, He's been there all the time, and that's a lot different than having to run to the Bible to check out the rules (if you can find one that applies).

One test to help you tell if you're really sharing your life with Jesus instead of with a rule book is this . . .

5. *Is my Christian life a case of "I must" or "I want"?*

In her book, *Going Steady with God,* Anna Mow writes: "Obeying God, no matter how we feel, is not the same as what some call 'legalistic obedience.' Legalistic obedience is obeying rules because we are afraid not to obey. It is like slave obedience—it is forced. It is 'I must, I must.' I had a . . . teacher who once said, 'Musts are awfully musty.' *Required obedience* is not Christian obedience. God does not make anyone 'be good.' Christian obedience is spontaneous obedience to a personal God who is like Jesus and springs from our love for Him. *Love makes us want to obey.*"[10]

To sum up, it's difficult to give up Christian games because games need rules and we seem to prefer rules and laws as ways to approach God. But Paul had little hope for game-playing. He said rules for legalistic games were only shadows of the real thing—Christ Himself (Col. 2:17). He thought the Colossian game-players were "proud men" with a vivid imagination, but ". . . not connected to Christ." (See Col. 2:18,19.) Paul knew, from personal experience, that winners of legalistic games are losers in the long run. To win these games doesn't make you a better person, it only makes you proud. (See Col. 2:23.)

Paul knew that a Christian life-style does not start with you and the rules, or what people advertise as the rules.* To be a Christian starts with you and Jesus Christ. You are joined to Him and you grow only as you get your nourishment and strength from Him. (See Col. 2:19 in *The Living Bible*.)

You can go beyond games—if you really want to. For some additional ideas read the next chapter.

TAKE A LOOK AT YOUR LIFE-STYLE

The Supernatural point of view . . .

Compare Col. 2:11,12 with Rom. 2:29; Phil.3:3; Rom. 6:1-8. According to these passages what is the real meaning of circumcision and baptism?

Compare Col. 2:13-15 with Eph. 2:1-10. Do you really believe a person is "dead in sin" before he knows Christ? How can a Christian be pardoned completely for sin by simply believing in Christ?

Compare Col. 2:20-23 with I Tim. 4:7,8. What does

---

*Rules for playing games and God's laws are two different things. See chapter 9.

101

Paul mean by ". . . discipline yourself for the purpose of godliness . . ."[a]? What is the difference between this kind of discipline and shaping up to please God as the Gnostics were teaching the Colossians to do?

Compare Col. 2:19 with Rom. 13:14. Do you agree with H. S. Vigeveno's comment on page 98 that the Christian is not able to keep any of his decisions?

If you'd like to do some further reading . . .

Games People Play, Dr. Eric Berne, Grove Press, 1964 (paperback edition, 1967), is written from a secular point of view, but has many applications to the spiritual life.

Sinners Anonymous, H. S. Vigeveno, Word Books, 1970, especially the chapter on "Legalists," p. 81.

Find Out for Yourself, Eugenia Price, Zondervan, 1963. See especially the chapter, "Finding Out about God."

Games Christians Play, Judi Culbertson and Patti Bard, Harper and Row, 1967, neatly punctures the legalistic and hypocritical balloons of religious pride.

Concerning games . . .

The adventurous life is not one exempt from fear . . . . Many people have the utopian idea that others are less afraid than they are, and they feel therefore that they are inferior. All men are afraid, even desperately afraid. . . . Fear is part of human nature.—Paul Tournier

. . . I am with you; that is all you need. My power shows up best in weak people . . .[b] (II Cor. 12:9).

Don't just sit there . . .

Review the five questions to help you go beyond

102

games; then write down possible games you might be playing (coin your own titles if you want). Put down ways you can go beyond these games to a freer, happier life.

Situation:

Game I'm playing:

What I will do:

Write your own prayer:

   "Lord, the Christian life-style I want is

CHAPTER 8

Heavenly-minded... EARTHLY GOOD?

Let's heaven fill your thoughts.
Paul

This world is not my home
I'm just a passin' through,
My treasures are laid up
Somewhere beyond the blue
The angels beckon me from heaven's open door
And I can't feel at home in this world anymore.

That old Christian song used to be popular, but you don't hear it much anymore. Somehow it doesn't fit in with the late twentieth century. Today the emphasis is on this world, society's ills, man's hang-ups. Heaven can wait. Besides, all the ecology crusades have made it clear that this world *is* our home and we are polluting it at record speeds.

Today is the day of the Now Generation. For many people heaven seems very very far away. The Now Generation is not too interested in what happened back *then*, or in what is going to happen *later*, because they are not too sure there is going to *be* a later.

To illustrate, a Now Generation collegian got into it with his Other Generation mother because he rejected a viewpoint that had always been sacred in the family (churchgoing perhaps?).

The argument waxed hotter and the two grew further and further apart. Things finally ground to a bewildering halt—especially for the mother—when her son, frustrated by his failure to communicate, put his hands on her shoulders and blurted, "Don't worry, the Jefferson Airplane loves you."[1]

The mother, of course, didn't know the Jefferson Airplane from the Spirit of St. Louis, which is sort of the point of the story. The Now Generation is wired for a different kind of sound, a different kind of talking. In the incredible upheaval and change of the late twentieth century, with social issues ranging from war, capital punishment and abortion to civil rights, campus unrest, and women's lib, how does a Christian use something like Col. 3:1-4 to construct a workable lifestyle?

"Since you became alive again, so to speak, when Christ arose from the dead, now set your sights on the rich treasures and joys of heaven where He sits beside God in the place of honor and power. Let heaven fill your thoughts; don't spend your time worrying about things down here. You should have as little desire for this world as a dead person does. Your real life is in heaven with Christ and God. And when Christ who is our real life comes back again, you will shine with Him and share in all His glories"[b] (Col. 3:1-4).

At first glance this looks like sheer religious escapism. Heaven fill your thoughts? A nice idea if you're a hermit maybe, but the rat race awaits you every Monday morning. Don't spend your time worrying about things down here? So what do you do about bills, your job, tests, term papers, dates, deadlines—ye almighty, relentless, ever present, pressure-packed SCHEDULE?

Colossians 3:1-4 doesn't seem to offer much help for developing an effective Christian life-style in an unchristian world. Maybe the best thing to do with this little paragraph is slip it under a big bookmark or put it in your file labeled, "Verses I must ask my minister about sometime."

On the other hand, these four little verses just might be one of the most important passages in all the New Testament. Here's why:

Colossians 3:1 refers back to Col. 2:11-12 where Paul talks about the difference between ritual circumcision and Christian baptism. When Paul says, "You are raised with Christ" he is trying to draw a picture of baptism with words. Baptism is an act of obedience signifying the believer's relationship to Christ, his identification with Christ's death and resurrection. When the believer is baptized he "dies" and then "rises again." As the waters close over the convert it is as though he is buried in death. When he comes up out of the water it is as if he has just "risen from the dead," into his new life as a Christian.

The Christian is to go on living in this world but from now on there is a big difference. To put it in terms discussed in the first six chapters of this book, the Christian no longer sees things from the Naturalist point of view, because now he's a Supernaturalist. The Naturalist lives as if this world is all there is and all that matters. The Christian lives in the knowledge that there is a larger Supernatural world that includes eternity and God. Paul is saying that we should set our sights (our mind) on things that are above, not on the world. We seek things that are above because that is where Christ is. If you want a Christian life-style keep your eyes on Christ. In chapters 1 and 2 of Colossians Paul talked a lot about *reconciliation*: how God brought us back to Himself. Here in chapter 3 he is talking about *sanctification*: how God changes us, makes us what He knows we can become.

Are you preoccupied with Christ?

In commenting on Col. 3:1-4 Bernard Ramm gives the opinion that the only route to sanctification is preoccupation with Jesus Christ and the things of Christ.[2]

You have probably heard comments like these more than once: "My work comes first." "Basketball is everything!" "Cars are where it's at!" "I'd rather ski than eat!"

A person's consuming interest—where he's investing his time, energy—helps reveal the kind of life-style he has chosen. For the Christian the ultimate is to be able to say, "Christ is my life, He dominates my thinking, He controls my desires. He is my motivation, my source of power."

All of which might sound like "instant sanctification." Just how does the Christian go about being "preoccupied with Christ" while handling earthly responsibilities and interests? Does getting sanctified mean you can't choose a career, that you can't be interested in sports, cars, etc.?

Following are some suggestions for developing a life-style that centers on Jesus Christ, but doesn't turn you into a hermit or religious escapist, so heavenly minded you're no earthly good. These ideas aren't too new, but they work:

1. *Stop playing "GUESS I'LL NEVER BE SPIRITUAL ENOUGH."*

Every Christian has played at least a few rounds of GINBSE. Everybody has his pet cop-out: "I'm too weak." "I'm easily tempted." "I've got old habits that

I'M SO WEAK... UNDISCIPLINED... ALWAYS TEMPTED... GOT BAD HABITS... HAD POOR EXAMPLES.

GUESS I'LL NEVER BE SPIRITUAL ENOUGH!

GINBSE IS A FOOLISH WASTE OF TIME . . .

are hard to break." "My parents set a poor example, so what do you expect from me?" (This is particularly effective if your parents are church pillars.)

GINBSE is a foolish waste of time. All you're doing is programming your mind with self-defeatism. Take positive, energy-building steps instead:

2. *Start each day with God's promises.*

Some people begin the day with no breakfast. They rather pride themselves on their ability to grab a cup of coffee, or nothing at all, and roar into the day's routine. But most nutrition experts (and almost all mothers) will tell you that breakfast is the most important meal of the day.

As important as breakfast is, how much more important it can be to pop a positive Biblical idea into your computer before starting another lap of the rat race. The words of Jesus are probably the best, but all parts of Scripture offer tremendous power because it is all God's Word for you.

Here are just a few of the many promises of God's Word that you can use to start each day. All are based on *The Living Bible;* some are paraphrased into the first person to make them extra personal for you.

With God, everything is possible (Matt. 19.26).

I can do everything God asks me to with the help of Christ (Phil. 4:13).

God will supply all that I need (Phil. 4:19).

God's mighty power at work in me is able to do far more than I dare to ask or dream (Eph. 3:20).

God is at work within me, helping me want to obey . . . (Phil. 2.13).

Anything is possible if I have faith (Mark 9:23).

Christ's words stand sure forever (Mark 13:31).

Ask and receive . . . seek and find . . . knock and the door opens (Luke 11:10).

I know the Truth and the Truth has set me free! (John 8:32).

I was blind, and now I see! (John 9:25).

Jesus gives me peace of mind and heart! (John 14:27).

If I really want God's will, I KNOW He's listening (I John 5:14, 15).

You can find many other promises, tailor-made for you, as you search God's Word for yourself.

3. *Use Christian psycho-cybernetics.*

A promise from God's Word gives you a good start in the right direction for the day, but don't leave it at that. Too many Christians think that "daily devotions" means seven minutes or half an hour in the Bible and at prayer. That's great, if you can hold yourself to it, but even this kind of daily discipline is not enough.

You can use the principles in what is called *psycho-cybernetics* to keep yourself on course all day long. Dr. Norbert Wiener and Dr. John Von Neumann used cybernetics during World War II to develop the steering

USE CHRISTIAN PSYCHO-CYBERNETICS TO GET ON TARGET AND STAY THERE.

mechanism in the torpedo. Torpedoes are equipped with a device that gives them "feedback" when they are off course. The device instantly corrects the path of the torpedo and it continues on toward its target.

The word *cybernetics* comes from a Greek word which is translated "steersman." Principles from the science of cybernetics have been applied to the human brain, hence the name, *psycho-cybernetics*. Dr. Maxwell Maltz, writing in his book, *Psycho-Cybernetics*, points out that while you are not a machine, your brain has many of the features and characteristics of a computer. You have a built-in servo-mechanism that can function as a guidance system to automatically steer you in the right direction to achieve certain goals.[3]

All you need is a target to shoot at. You need to see this target clearly in your mind. If you are serious about setting your sights on heaven and being preoccupied with Christ, you've got your target. You can keep yourself on course through the day by repeating positive Biblical ideas of what you want to be and what you are in Christ.

Use the promises mentioned above, not only for "day openers" but repeat them to yourself as you go through your daily routine. Use them in all kinds of situations: when the going is easy or tough; when things are dull or exciting; when you're feeling high or low. Repeat them to yourself no matter how ridiculous they might sound at the time. People have literally talked themselves out of divorce, suicide, depression, you name it, by repeating positive ideas.[4]

If mere human reasoning is capable of this, consider the possibilities in opening yourself to the work of the Holy Spirit through the light of God's Word.

Keep telling yourself you've had it with Christian life, with the church, with phony Christians, and you have. Keep telling yourself you want God to really run your life and heaven to fill your thoughts and it will happen.

Here are some more promises you can use:

Jesus *does* love me (John 15:9).

He cares about *everything* I'm doing (Matt. 10:29-31).

Nothing can come between me and Jesus
        (Rom. 8:38, 39).

I'm *becoming* what God wants me to be (Rom. 5:2).

Nothing can stop me (Phil. 4:13).

4. *Practice selective computer programming.*

The old cliché says, "You are what you eat." Even more true is: "You are what you *think*." Since your brain can be programmed like a computer, it makes sense to be a little fussy about what goes into your mind through eye and ear (not to mention nose, throat, and veins in this day of so-called better living through chemistry).

Being "selective" doesn't mean that you run a 24-hour censoring bureau. The average person operating in high school, college, the business world, or any other secular environment, would soon find himself rating life

IF YOU GIGGLE, BLUSH, GET UP TIGHT OR TURNED ON WITH PLAIN OLD UNADULTERATED LUST BY WHAT YOU ARE READING, SEEING, HEARING, YOU CAN USUALLY BE SURE YOU ARE BEING PROGRAMMED IN THE WRONG WAY.

with a big "X". You can't live in an unchristian world with a glass bubble over your head, but there is one good "taste test" for the kind of stuff you get hit with in books, TV, movies, magazines and even "casual conversation."

If you giggle, blush, get up-tight or turned on with plain old unadulterated lust, by what you are reading, seeing or hearing, you can usually be sure you are being programmed in the wrong way. If, however, you can analyze it according to Biblical principles and Christ-implanted values, you can probably handle it.*

But a word of caution. Don't go looking for the racy, the questionable, the spicy. If you're normal, you'll get more than your share of that without even trying. Instead, take Paul's advice: "Fix your thoughts on what is true and good and right. Think about things that are pure and lovely, and dwell on the fine, good things in others. Think about all you can praise God for and be glad about"ᵇ (Phil. 4:8).

5. *Always keep on praying.*

That means pray for it, because of it, about it,

*Please read this little test again. It contains two *very* big *if's*.

112

through it, around it or in spite of it. This isn't easy. It takes real stamina. Most of us are good at praying *for* it. Some of us pray *because* of it. And we piously tell people we'll pray *about* it. But few of us pray *through* it or in *spite* of it.

Prayer just might be the most neglected, poorly executed art in all Christendom. Yet it is the key to letting heaven fill your thoughts. As Paul put it in Phil. 4:6: "Don't worry about anything; instead, pray about everything. . . ."⁵ (For more on this, see chapter 12, "Let's Pray About It (For a Change)."

6. *Stay on target to take off the pressure.*

Everybody is pretty well agreed that this old world is a real pressure cooker. The clock and the calendar started out as servants, but in the late twentieth century they have turned into tyrants.

Because of earthly pressures—to produce, perform, come through, knuckle under, etc., it really makes sense to set your mind on Christ. He keeps you on target because He *is* the target. He is the unifying effect in your life. He gives you the goal for living as a Christian in this unchristian world.

Keith Miller, whose books are must reading if you're serious about being a Christian in an unchristian world, writes in *Habitation of Dragons* about how a goal can unify your life. In high school he wanted to be an all-American basketball player. Having this "single dominant incentive" gave him a way to establish priorities. It turned out that all-American was out of Miller's reach, but it didn't matter. Having that goal helped him tie together many loose ends in his life during a time when he could have wound up the way a lot of people (young and old) wind up: with two or three dozen irons in the fire and none of them very hot.

Miller applies his teen-age goal of basketball superstar to his Christian life (which didn't start until he was married and into the business world). He has discovered that as he commits his life to finding Christ's purposes for him that ". . . my energies and abilities are gradually being focused and are working together."

Miller admits that sometimes he wants to play games instead. He suffers from "goal schizophrenia": wanting to serve Christ and wanting his own ego trip. But when this happens he stops, reevaluates, begins again, and finds a beautiful paradox. He is free to pursue his earthly goals and responsibilities because his ultimate happiness does not depend on succeeding there anymore. He says, ". . . what a relief it is to have found a unifying adventure in the Christian life . . . because it certainly is."[5]

During the revolutions and changing times of the sixties and seventies, Christians have been getting lots of heat for being so heavenly minded they're no earthly good. To hear some tell it, Christians are personally responsible for everything from war and poverty to pollution and prejudice. Some of this criticism is right on target (and a lot of it isn't) but that is not really the point. Getting involved in social issues to get rid of a guilt complex (or just sitting around feeling guilty and staying uninvolved) is no answer for living as a Christian in an unchristian world.

Instead, you need something to make your Christian life a unifying adventure, and Paul talks about that something in Col. 3:1-4. Some Christians may squirm when an unchristian world says, "You Christians and your pie in the sky . . . heaven can wait . . . live it up while you're still able."

But for the Christian, heaven *can't* wait.

Setting your sights on heaven . . . letting heaven fill your thoughts . . . having as little desire for this world as a dead person does. . . .

These are not hatches of religious escapism that lead

you inward to being so concerned with your "spirituality," you are indifferent to suffering, injustice and evil. They are *doors that open out,* into a life of meaning, purpose and release.

TAKE A LOOK AT YOUR LIFE-STYLE

The Supernatural point of view . . .

Compare Col. 3:1-4 with II Pet. 1:4 and II Cor. 3:18 (use *The Living Bible* or Phillips translation if at all possible). How does being in process—being transformed by God—make you feel? What results can you already see? What do you hope for?

Compare Col. 3:1-4 with Matt. 5:1-16; Matt. 6:25-34; Phil. 3:19,20; Titus 2:12; James 4:4; Rom. 12:1,2. Then write down your definition of "worldliness" and how you intend to deal with it in your life.

Compare Col. 3:1-4 with II Cor. 5:14-21. Paul says the Christian no longer lives for himself, but for the One who died for his sake. List three things you are now doing (or will start doing) because you no longer live for yourself, but for Christ.

If you'd like to do some further reading . . .

Move Ahead with Possibility Thinking, Robert H. Schuller, Doubleday and Company, 1967. Written by the pastor of the famed Garden Grove (California) Drive-In Church. Full of practical suggestions and inspiring anecdotes.

Psycho-Cybernetics: The New Way to a Successful Life, Maxwell Maltz, Prentice-Hall, 1960. An excellent framework for personality development when built on the foundation of Scripture.

Still Higher for His Highest, Oswald Chambers, Zondervan, 1970 is a sequel to Chambers' well-known, *My*

Utmost for His Highest. He is not "light devotional reading." You may or may not be ready for him.

Concerning goals . . .

The IS must never catch up with the OUGHT. —Dr. Viktor Frankl

Blessed are the single-hearted, for they shall enjoy much peace.—Thomas a Kempis

He died for all so that all who live—having received eternal life from Him—might live no longer for themselves, to please themselves, but to spend their lives pleasing Christ who died and rose again for them. —II Cor. 5:15, *The Living Bible*

Don't just sit there . . .

After reading this chapter, what are some goals you can set for yourself? What can you start doing, *right now?* Write something here, no matter how simple or small it might seem to be:

Write your own prayer . . .
"Lord, my life's goal is

CHAPTER 9

ARE YOU A THERMOMETER OR THERMOSTAT?

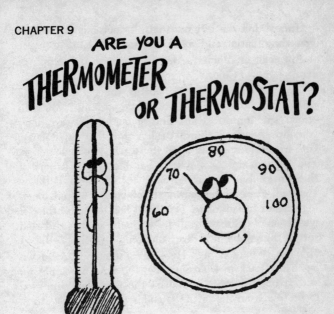

"All formulas, rules and regulations, should be left unsaid. All decisions depend to some extent on the individual and the situation and his relationship to God. There are no pat answers."

When it comes to "real life" this comment, by an anonymous coed at a New Jersey school,[1] sounds quite wise and with it. You certainly have to agree that, today especially, *there are no pat answers.*

Why, even Paul might concur. According to what he says in Col. 2:16-23, he is down on rules, regulations and playing games to earn Christian brownie points (see chapter 7). And in Col. 3:1-4, he is up on relating to Christ and letting heaven fill your thoughts (see chapter 8).

And, didn't the girl say that all decisions depend on you, the situation and *your relationship to God?*

But wait . . . what's this in the next paragraph of Paul's letter to Colosse? . . .

"Away then with sinful, earthly things; deaden the evil desires lurking within you; have nothing to do with sexual sin, impurity, lust and shameful desires; don't worship the good things of life, for that is idolatry. God's terrible anger is upon those who do such things. You used to do them when your life was still part of this world; but now is the time to cast off and throw away all these rotten garments of anger, hatred, cursing and dirty language. Don't tell lies to each other; it was your old life with all its wickedness that did that sort of thing; now it is dead and gone'" (Col. 3:5-9).

What is Paul doing? He just finished putting down legalism (back in Colossians 2) and now he comes up with a big list of no-no's. Isn't the Christian supposed to be free from the law? the codes? the life of legalistic games?

Joseph Fletcher, a leading advocate of what is called "situation ethics," has gone to great lengths in his writing and speaking to assure Christians they are free from all laws—except for the one he calls the "law of love." In brief, Joseph Fletcher says:

The only thing that really matters in life is love. You should always distribute your love according to what you decide is most loving in those circumstances, and never allow a list of prescribed rules or laws to be the final authority for making your decisions. You might consult lists of laws and rules, but you have the last word.*

*For a complete presentation of Fletcher's views, read his books *Situation Ethics: The New Morality,* Westminster Press, Copyright 1966. Also see Fletcher's book, *Moral Responsibility: Situation Ethics at Work,* Westminster Press, Copyright 1967.

All of this sounds very much like the coed whose comment opened this chapter. Forget the formulas, rules and regulations and let the individual work out his own decision according to the situation and "his relationship to God." For Joseph Fletcher the Ten Commandments aren't a list of authoritative laws. In fact, he says that "For the situationist there are no rules—none at all." If situation ethics "has any rules, they are only rules of thumb."²

Joseph Fletcher's situational ethic seems to make perfectly good sense. It sounds so *mature*, so *responsible*, so *free* to say you want to make each moral decision according to what is "most loving for *that* situation." It all sounds like a perfect way to go beyond a life of legalistic games.

Except for one fairly important item.

You aren't perfect (i.e., God).

Situation ethics is a trap for two reasons

1. *It leads to moral and ethical dead ends.* There is always the sticky problem of coming to some situations and *not wanting* to do the loving thing or *not being able* to. Fletcher almost ignores the problem of sin, which all of us still have to cope with. Without moral absolutes the practice of situational morality, with each person doing his own loving thing, quickly turns into a sick, very confused joke. Because Fletcher accurately labels legalism as sick and confused does not make his system the answer.

2. *Situation ethics leads to spiritual dead ends.* Intimacy with Christ*—living in Him and He in you—does not make you autonomous; indeed you don't want to be. For the Christian who takes the Bible seriously

*See chapter 7, pp. 99-100 and chapter 8, pp. 110-115.

(not, in Fletcher's terms, as "rules of thumb") the existence of the Big Absolute—Jesus Christ—leads to other absolutes or the concept of "absolute" means little.

Of course, Paul tells the Colossians to cool it on dirty sex, cheating, hating, filthy talk. These and similar pastimes are definitely no-no's because of the big YES—Jesus Christ.

As Paul puts it: "You are living a brand new kind of life that is continually learning more and more of what is right, and trying constantly to be more and more like Christ who created this new life within you"ᵇ (Col. 3:10).

To this most Christians reply: "Yes, that's what I want . . . a new kind of life-style . . . to learn more of what is right . . . to be like Jesus Himself. But . . . HOW? Just what is morality? What makes someone or something moral or immoral?"

According to Webster, to be immoral is to fail to conform to a standard of what is good and right. Scripture says the same thing, but in more graphic terms: "All have sinned; all fall short of God's glorious ideal"ᵇ (Rom. 3:23).

Scripture defines sin in an active sense: "Everyone who practices sin also practices lawlessness; and sin is lawlessness"ᵃ (I John 3:4); and in a passive sense: "Therefore, to one who knows the right thing to do, and does not do it, to him it is sin"ᵃ (James 4:17).

If you wanted to sum it all up in one sentence, you could say:

"Immorality is the use and/or abuse of God and others in a selfish, calculating, unloving way."

But what about those sticky situations?

As explicit as the Bible is about immorality, it still sounds too general for some people. They want to know: *What* is selfish? *What* is calculating and unloving? *What* is impure? *What* is dirty? After all, struggles in the courts have suggested that one man's pornography can be another man's "appreciation of fine art." What then does the Christian do with the sticky, neither black nor white, situations?

Following is one suggestion for making a systematic stab at the sticky decisions—in fact—at all ethical decisions that you face daily. This "system" provides no pat answers. There is no guarantee that you will always have the right answer for every situation. But what these five specific questions can do is help you evaluate the situation, analyze it, take it apart and get a better perspective based on God's wisdom, not just your own. If Supernatural Christianity includes anything, it includes the promise that the Christian has "the mind of Christ." (See I Cor. 2:9-16.)

1. *"Am I being a thermometer or thermostat?"*

One of the greatest challenges to being a Christian in an unchristian world is to handle the morals and ethics of your peer group—that is, not letting *them* handle *you*. Do you let other people run your life more than you might care to admit? If so, you are an ethical *thermometer* capable only of reacting to your environment. You have no inner strength, no moral self-starter mechanism. Church may make you pious; but when you are around godless people you can suddenly become profane, or at least a lot more tactful about sounding or looking too religious.

You say you don't run with "that kind of crowd"? It's still easy enough to be a thermometer. Return evil for evil (chop for chop, etc.), and you are plastic, motivated by the circumstances. Repay bitterness with bitterness and you are just as out of control as the other person. There are countless ways the environment can

WHEN FACING STICKY DECISIONS... ASK

THERMOMETER
OR
THERMOSTAT?

WHAT'S FAIR AND
LOVING?

WHAT IS MY DUTY?

WHAT DOES THE
BIBLE SAY?

CHRIST OR THE
CROWD?

make your ethical life go up and down just like the temperature on a thermometer.

Of course if you don't like the idea of other people running your life or controlling it, you can let God run your life. Then, instead of being a thermometer you can be a *thermostat*. You can have a control center of power and strength that helps you determine and create conditions, not just respond to them.

So, the first thing you need to decide in any situation is which decision will make you act like a thermometer and which will make you act like a thermostat? In this unchristian world, if you aren't interested in trying to be a thermostat, you might as well forget it when it comes to practicing Christian ethics.[3]

2. *"What is the fair and loving thing to do in this situation?"*

Who is really going to benefit from the decision you make? All questions of ethics and morals start here. Everybody is pretty well agreed on wanting fair play. Everybody wants justice—at least for himself.

Joseph Fletcher's *Situation Ethics* is built on this question. This is where he starts. Trouble is, he doesn't go much farther and Christian morality lies somewhere beyond. Don't bypass this question, however, and take it for granted. One reason a lot of Christians aren't too convincing to an unchristian world is that when it comes right down to it, they don't always play that fair.

3. *"What is my duty—moral obligation? Do I even care about my duty in this situation?"*

With this question things get a little tighter. You are starting to think about what kind of a person you really are—on the inside. You must face yourself and ask yourself if you even want to be fair and loving in making this decision, whatever it might be.

Joseph Fletcher puts heavy emphasis on "doing the

123

loving thing within the situation." He makes a strong plea for a sense of responsibility and a mature facing up to the difficulties in life. But Fletcher's heavy emphasis on autonomously deciding for yourself about what is loving leaves you in a leaking ethical boat. It is interesting to note that in his book, *Situation Ethics,* Fletcher does not have the word *sin* in the index. A reading of the book will bear out that sin just doesn't come up that often. When everyone is free to decide for himself what the "loving thing" is, it is easy to confuse duty with self-interest. Christian morality lies still farther down the ethical path. . . .

4. *"What do the Scriptures teach concerning this situation—in general or in particular?"*

Joseph Fletcher would say that all the Scriptures teach is "the law of love." Fletcher believes that the two great commandments of Christ (see Matt. 22:37-39) are a distillation—"That the essential spirit and ethos of many laws has been distilled or liberated, extracted, filtered out, with the legal husks, or rubbish, thrown away as dross."[4]

Fletcher then goes on to grind up a few of these "husks," namely the Ten Commandments. By the time Fletcher gets through, you are left feeling apprehensive about reading the Bible too much, lest you become what he calls a legalist. By legalists, Fletcher really means "those who disagree with my theology."

In a debate with Fletcher,* conservative theologian John Warwick Montgomery said ". . . it is manifestly clear that Professor Fletcher's understanding of love and morality does not derive from the Bible in general or from Jesus' ministry in particular . . . moreover, his

---

*In this same debate, held on the San Diego State College campus in February 1971, Fletcher made the remark that Jesus was a Jewish peasant with no more philosophical sophistication than a guinea pig.

acceptance of radical techniques of New Testament criticism removes any real possibility of his identifying the ethic of Jesus: were he to take the entire New Testament picture seriously, he would find—as any number of his critics have shown—that the New Testament, no less than the Old, insists on absolute moral standards."[5]

As the brief look at Col. 2:16-23 (chapter 7, pp. 89-103) revealed, "legalism" is a matter of putting man-made rules, traditions and concerns ahead of God's Word. That's what the Gnostics were doing at Colosse. That's what the Pharisees were doing when Jesus put them in their place (Matt. 23:13-36). If you are enjoying a deepening relationship with Christ (spiritual intimacy) it follows that you will be in God's Word. Christ will be guiding and molding your life through His Holy Spirit. There is no better way to escape legalism, because in truth the legalist is the one who is far from Christ trying to exist on his own power, and above all, on his own merit.

As for being able to know what the Scriptures say—in general or particular—about ethical problems you face, all kinds of lists of Scripture verses on "what to do if . . ." are available, but it is far better to program your computer (brain) with God's Word continually. Christian morality is not so much a case of being able to punch the right ethical button and come up with the precise solution each and every time; it is more a case of hearing the still small voice of the Holy Spirit as He tells you what is right or wrong.

5. *"Which choice in this situation will strengthen my relationship to Christ? Which choice will weaken it?"*

Jesus said, "You can know the Truth (Me) and I will make you free" (see John 8:32). The key to understanding this is to realize that Jesus doesn't offer *freedom from* restraints, or even laws and rules. Naturalist man wants a freedom of no restraints, no laws and no rules—because he thinks this world is all there is and that he is (or should be) in charge of his own life.

But for the Christian Jesus offers *freedom to*. This is a Supernatural freedom to live in God's world, to become what He created you to be.

Jesus also said, "The one who obeys Me is the one who loves Me . . ."[b] (John 14:21). Freedom in Christ means obedience to Christ. There are many differences between a stinking, slimy swamp and a clear rushing river. One big difference is that the river has borders (restraints), and the swamp has none.[6]

It isn't easy to stay out of the ethical swamps. Swamps have many confusing turns, twists and dead ends. One thing is for sure: you will never find your way out of the ethical swamp if you follow the ever-lovin' crowd. Most of the crowd likes it in the swamp. They like the freedom of "no restraints," or so they tell themselves.

But swamps are full of quicksand, not to mention snakes and alligators. To live without "restraints" isn't freedom. It is the worst kind of slavery with self as the master.

The Christian's Master is Jesus Christ. We submit to His authority (not authoritarianism) and by submitting we find (as He promised) that we are free indeed! (See John 8:36.)

John Stott illustrates freedom in submission by pointing out that "To express himself freely, a pianist must accept the discipline that the keyboard imposes on him. His greatest flights of freedom and self-expression are not in defiance of this but in submission to it."[7]

Stott goes on to say that he ". . . finds freedom in knowing God's Mind, thinking God's Thoughts after Him. My will finds its freedom in obeying God's Will— doing God's Thing, not my thing."[8]

126

And that brings you right back to the first question: thermometer or thermostat? If you commit yourself to being a thermostat, you will be an instrument that determines and creates better moral conditions. But there's more to it than that. A thermostat needs energy of some kind to operate. The mighty energy at work within the Christian is the Holy Spirit—the One whom Christ has sent to live in and empower all Christians. It is the Holy Spirit who takes you beyond mere wishful thinking about love and fair play. He can give you the desire to want to be fair and loving. He can guide you into all truth. (See John 16:13.) He will tell you what is taking you away from Christ and what is bringing you closer to Him.

Questions concerning morals and ethics come from everywhere: to lust or not to lust . . . to bed or not to bed . . . to hate and lie or love and tell the truth . . . to worship power and self (idolatry) or worship God.

Your only chance to be a thermostat in a world choking on thermometers is to take God's Word for it: "You are living a brand new kind of life that is continually learning more and more of what is right, and trying constantly to be more and more like Christ who created this new life within you."

TAKE A LOOK AT YOUR LIFE-STYLE

The Supernatural point of view . . .

Morality involves much more than sex. It involves all kinds of behavior, as Col. 3:5-9 points out. According to Bible scholar William Barclay, Paul's talk about "mortifying the flesh" and "deadening evil desires lurking within" is not an invitation to religious aesthetic fanaticism. Barclay quotes C.F.D. Moule who says *the Christian must kill self-centeredness.*[9]

The motive for killing self-centeredness is **Christ.** Verses like Gal. 5:16; I Pet. 2:11; 4:2; James 4:1 make good sense when compared with Matt. 16:24; Rom. 8:12-14; Gal. 5:24.

So, when Scripture warns against *fornication and adultery* (I Thess. 4:3-7; Matt. 5:27-29) *coveting* (Exod. 20:17; Jer. 6:13), *anger* (Matt. 5:22), *slander* (I Pet. 2:1), just to name a few, the purpose is not to saddle Christians with legalistic burdens but to warn them against the quicksand of self-centeredness that can so easily suck you under—into a life of using (and abusing) others, rather than loving them.

Scripture mentions a lot of no-no's because of the Big Yes—Jesus Christ. Col. 3:10 says the Christian is a *new man* (II Cor. 5:17; Eph. 4:21-24), *renewed through the Holy Spirit* (Rom. 12:12; Titus 3:5), *possessor of spiritual knowledge* (John 7:16,17; 8:31,32), and *remade in the image of his Creator—Christ* (II Cor. 3:18; I John 3:2).

If you'd like to do some further reading...

See Book III, "Christian Behavior" in C. S. Lewis' matchless apologetic, *Mere Christianity*, Macmillan. Lewis' discussion of "The Three Parts of Morality" was a major resource for chapter 9.

For more on situation ethics, see *The Other Side of Morality*, Regal Books, 1969, chapters 1-5, for an analysis of Joseph Fletcher's system.

It's a Playboy World, William Banowsky, Revell, 1969 is a penetrating analysis of the hedonistic philosophy that grips much of secular society today.

Concerning morals...

Fire proves iron, and temptation a just man.
—Thomas a Kempis

Temptation is an irresistible force at work on a movable body.—H. L. Mencken

The mind is dyed the color of its habitual thoughts. —Marcus Aurelius

Don't just sit there . . .

Following are some typical remarks a Christian could hear or make himself. Each remark sets up a possible situation for moral decision making. Evaluate each comment in light of the five questions discussed in this chapter and summed up in the cartoon on p. 122.

"Oh come on, you can have one drink, can't you?"

"What's the harm? They never check the register."

"He's just a vegetable, why not turn off the machine and save everyone a lot of trouble?"

"Margaret Mead says premarital sex can prevent divorce later . . . don't you love me?"

"Why can't you go see 'Pretty Maids All in a Row'?"

"Yes, it's my brother's last clean shirt, but this date I've got tonight is really *heavy*."

"She's been really sick and old Harkness is making no exceptions . . . should I let her have a few answers?"

"Why shouldn't Kathy and I live together for a while? Marriage can wait until we see if she pulls out of her drug habit. We know what we're doing . . . we want a responsible relationship."

Write your own prayer. Lord, help me be a thermostat regarding . . .

CHAPTER 10

PEOPLE OR PERSONS

Describe in 25 words or so the ideal Christian class, group, church, family. What would it be like? What characteristics . . . virtues . . . atmosphere . . . would be present?

Perhaps you would need a lot more than 25 words. On the other hand, how many words would you need for *your* class, group, church, family? Following is Paul's description . . .

"You are living a brand new kind of life that is continually learning more and more of what is right, and trying constantly to be more and more like Christ who created this new life within you. In this new life one's nationality or race or education or social position is unimportant; such things mean nothing. Whether a person has Christ is what matters, and He is equally available to all.

"Since you have been chosen by God who has given you this new kind of life, and because of His deep love and concern for you, you should practice tenderhearted mercy and kindness to others. Don't worry about making a good impression on them but be ready to suffer quietly and patiently. Be gentle and ready to forgive; never hold grudges. Remember, the Lord forgave you, so you must forgive others. Most of all, let love guide your life, for then the whole church will stay together in perfect harmony. Let the peace of heart which comes from Christ be always present in your hearts and lives, for this is your responsibility and privilege as members of His body. And always be thankful'" (Col. 3:10-15).

As mentioned in chapter 9, Paul stresses the need for a certain amount of negative Christianity in Col. 3:5-9, where he is dealing with what Bernard Ramm calls ". . . root sins . . . not . . . cultural superficials.'" But here in Col. 3:10-15, he goes on to talk about the positives —and paints a picture of what "being spiritual" (sanctified) is all about. At the same time he is describing "the ideal Christian community" and how it functions. Paul is saying that Christians who are serious about Christ and living a brand new kind of life (v. 10) should possess certain qualities, which become especially evident when they are together.

He reminds the Colossian Christians that position or profession means nothing (v. 11). Having Christ is what counts. They are God's chosen ones and *because of God's love for them* they should practice a substantial list of Christian virtues. It's interesting to note that Paul doesn't mention qualities such as cleverness, efficiency or even diligence. Paul keeps talking about basics, the

WE THINK CHRISTIAN VIRTUES ARE WORTHY AND DESIRABLE, BUT SOME OF THEM SEEM A BIT TOO IDEALISTIC FOR US TO ATTAIN.

nitty-gritty things in human relationships: mercy, kindness, humility, meekness, patience, forgiveness, love, peace.[2]

Now surely the virtues Paul mentions here are worthy and desirable. We all say we want to practice them (and surely we want to have them practiced *on us*).

Some virtues, such as mercy and kindness (v. 12), are simple enough. At least we have an idea of how to attain them—or how we fail to attain them. In families, groups, churches—whatever the organization—we pass up countless little opportunities every day to be merciful and kind to one another and we pay for it in the dry rot that eats away at our relationships.

But humility and meekness (v. 12), sounds a bit unreal, too idealistic and "Christian" to work in the rat race of competitive life. A hang-up that many Christians have about humility is that they think it is supposed to signify some superspiritual depreciation of one's self. We like to joke about how we will someday write a book entitled, "Christian Humility and How I Attained It," but actually we aren't sure that Christian humility is attainable or particularly desirable. We know we are too proud, but servile groveling in a mudhole of inadequacy and imperfection seems to be no answer at all. Our very awareness of our sin and our pride makes us feel that this kind of cringing confession is hypocritical and phony.

One problem for a lot of people is wanting too much. They are too self-conscious about their need to win their share of heats in the social rat race. They want recognition, a reputation, popularity—all of which are great ego expanders. Paradoxically, they miss the sheer wonder and joy in having a simple dream and pursuing it with naive enthusiasm.

A devastating 6.6 earthquake rocked the Los Angeles, California area on February 9, 1971. On February 13, the following story appeared in the *Los Angeles Times:*

At 10, Angel Ferrer stood only 4 feet tall and weighed 59 pounds, but he dreamed a dream with more intensity than many bigger boys could muster: He wanted to be a Cub Scout. But the $3.50 registration fee couldn't be squeezed from his family's welfare budget. But Angel clung to his dream. He collected old pop bottles and aluminum cans and saved up 53 cents.

He used the money to buy a used Cub Scout uniform at the Salvation Army store. It was baggy and tattered and had unfaded spots where someone else's badges were once sewn, but it was "regulation." Still without the registration fee, Angel and his father Julio went to a Cub pack meeting on January 28. "The little kid sat there in his uniform and watched everything like a thirsty man looks at water," the pack leader, policeman Richard Jesson, recalls.

"We made plans to take Angel on our next camping trip." They went, Cub Scout Pack 44 and Angel. "You should have seen that kid on our trip," recalls Jesson. "He was the first in line for everything and did everything 3 times harder than anyone else. The poor little guy didn't have a sleeping bag or regulation mess kit like everyone else. He brought all he had—a regular dinner plate, a plastic fork, and a plastic cup."

The pack returned home February 7, and for 2 days, all Angel talked about was the outing. The southern California earthquake came, and San Fernando, where Angel lived, was one of the communities hardest hit. He died. Angel was to have received merit badges in front of the other boys of Pack 44 in 2 weeks. Instead, a funeral director pinned them on the coffin. Angel's Cub Scout uniform looked new—it was. Angel's parents had bought it only 4 hours before the funeral.[3]

The Angel Ferrer story isn't supposed to imply that Cub Scouting is equal to being a Christian, but somehow it catches the spirit of what humility means. Pride is thinking too much of yourself or about yourself. Humility is being so aware of something or someone outside yourself that you forget about your "dignity," importance, image. For Angel, his something—his focal point—was Cub Scouting.

Christian humility is something like this. . . . It is an awareness that you are a creature—the creation of God. It is also an awareness that all men are creatures created by God and the pride that puts one person above another is one of the deadliest of sins. Recipes for cutting down on your pride and building genuine humility can be found in James 4:1-10 and I Pet. 5:1-11. James and Peter both base their remarks on Prov. 3:34—on the awareness that humility is a matter of living close enough to God to let Him help you tell the difference between having the right self-image and taking a continual ego trip.

Meekness is another virtue that puzzles us. Again we are not sure what it means to be meek or even if we want to be meek. Meekness makes us think of Casper Milquetoast, not exactly our favorite model. But our problem is the same as it is with humility. We don't understand what meekness means.

Moses was called "meek" and so was Jesus. Neither man exactly fits the Casper Milquetoast description. To be meek is to be open, acceptant, willing to receive whatever God or others have for you. James talks about receiving the implanted Word of God with meekness (James 1:21). Meekness is not for Casper Milquetoasts; neither is it for the cocky, the overconfident, the all-self-sufficient ones. Meekness is a trait of those with enough courage to yield themselves to God.

As *The Living Bible* puts it, when you are meek you are ". . . ready to suffer quietly and patiently"[b] (v. 12). Impatience is what you might call the fuse that leads to the dynamite of anger (or at least irritability). Patience is the quality of "hanging in there" no matter how obnoxious, discouraging, or exasperating people and events may become.

The Africans have a proverb that says it pretty well: "With patience you can dig a well with a needle."

Forgiveness (v. 13) is a key Christian virtue, because forgiveness is what Christianity is all about. It all started when God forgave us.

Most people should be wearing a sign: "Fragile feelings, handle with care." But we don't always handle others with care. We are clumsy, unconcerned and prone to make mistakes. Mistakes have done more to cause wars, break up marriages, riddle friendships and split groups, churches and organizations than anything else. But mistakes aren't what really do it. It is the lack of forgiveness for the mistakes. Prov. 17:9 reminds us

135

that "love forgets mistakes."⁵ Without love you can't forget mistakes, nor can you be patient, meek, humble or kind or merciful. Perhaps that is why Paul goes on to say, "And beyond all these things put on love, which is the perfect bond of unity"ª (v. 14). Love isn't something you "turn on" or use as part of a do-it-yourself-kit for better human relations. Love is the glue to help people stick together and work together in harmony.

Love is the mark of "living in Christ." (See I John 2:6.) Christ told us to love one another as *He had loved us*. (See John 13:34,35.) So the first question is not, "Do we love one another?" The first question is, "Do we love Christ?" and are we willing to let Him bind us together? If we do, we will have *peace* (v. 15), and by this Paul means the peace of Christ.

Unless Christ is calling the close ones . . .

According to the Greek text, Paul is literally saying that we should let the peace of God be *umpire* in our hearts. The word comes direct from the athletic arena. It refers to the one who settles the close and difficult plays with his decisions. It can get quite hectic on a baseball diamond, a basketball court, a football field, or wherever a game is being played. It can also get quite hectic in a church, a family, a group, or an organization. If Christ isn't calling the close ones and if all sides aren't willing to abide by His decisions, there can be no ball game.⁕

Paul lists some eight or nine Christian virtues, and as you read them you find yourself saying, "How nice . . . but isn't it all a little impossible? Paul didn't have to

⁕Reference here to athletic games and letting Christ be umpire in your hearts is not to be confused with the psychological games talked about in chapter 7. Athletic contests are to be played fairly, with equal chance to win for both sides. Psychological games are never played fairly because the players want to win at any price.

live with *my* family, *my* church, *my* organization." No, Paul didn't. He just had to live with the hatred of the Jews who followed him around on his missionary journeys throwing *real* stones at him. He had to live with such "spirit-filled groups" as the church at Corinth, where (for a while at least) he was practically burned in effigy every Sunday. He just had to live with ignorance, immaturity and insincerity in almost every church he helped start. And, he had to live with his own propensity to come on too strong, to lean on people a little too hard.

In Col. 3:10-15, Paul lists Christian virtues—targets that all Christians should aim at daily. Then he gives some practical suggestions for hitting those targets . . .

"Remember what Christ taught and let His words enrich your lives and make you wise; teach them to each other and sing them out in psalms and hymns and spiritual songs, singing to the Lord with thankful hearts. And whatever you do or say, let it be as a representative of the Lord Jesus, and come with Him into the presence of God the Father to give Him your thanks"[b] (Col. 3:16,17).

It's important to note that these suggestions aren't a "psychological success scheme." Everything Paul says is centered directly on Christ. It is only from Christ you get the power to possess and live out Christian virtues. You don't learn Christian virtues and say, "This is how I am becoming sanctified—more and more yielded to Christ." As you become sanctified, Christian virtues are the *results*.

First, Paul talks about letting Christ's words enrich your life, or in the vernacular, "turn you on." And as Jesus turns you on, you can turn on others by sharing with them, teaching them, as Paul says, with psalms, hymns and spiritual songs. The title song of the folk musical, *Natural High*, nicely sums up what Col. 3:16

is saying about sharing what you have learned and experienced in Christ:

> It's a scientific formula, effectively reduced
> To simple terms so everyone can try.
> It's a perfectly legal, non-chemically induced,
> Logically 'natural high.'
> Just turn on your mind to wisdom,
> Turn on your heart to love.
> Turn on your soul but natural,
> Turn on to God above.
> Turn on your eyes to kindness,
> Turn on your dreams to give.
> Turn on your strength to help someone,
> Turn on to God and live.*

But Paul saves the best for last. Col. 3:17 could be called *sanctification in a nutshell* or *the shortest handbook on morality ever written.* "Whatever you do or say," says Paul, "let it be as a representative of the Lord Jesus. . . ."[b]

Life constantly presents its big and little hang-ups—those sticky situations that arise to confront you with choices where it is hard to see the difference between self-interest and the so-called right thing to do. You can't have a ready-made answer book for everything. One group that tried hard to do this was the Pharisees, and they were a sorry sight to behold, as Jesus pointed out time and again (Matt. 23:13-28, Mark 7:1-13). So instead of having a little rule book you carry around for every situation, you need a standard. The Christian standard is simply, "Can I do this in Christ's name?"

One problem with this, however, is that it seems to give too simple an answer to complex questions. In today's unchristian world you invariably will find your-

---

A Natural High by Ralph Carmichael. Copyright 1969 by LEXICON MUSIC, INC. All rights reserved. International copyright secured. Used by special permission.

HOW TO HAVE A NATURAL HIGH

LET JESUS TURN YOU ON!

TEACH EACH OTHER

DO ALL IN CHRIST'S NAME

THANK GOD FOR EVERYTHING YOU DO

self in situations that don't necessarily look too spiritual, too uplifting. You may have to work with people who don't have your Christian point of view or your value-system. Sometimes it seems that if you are going to be consistent about being a representative of Christ in everything you do or say, the only thing to do is to become a vegetable growing in a Christian hothouse where the big bad world can't touch you.

That is *not* what Paul has in mind. In the second half of verse 17 he says that as you do and say things as Christ's representative you are to ". . . come with Him into the presence of God the Father to give Him your thanks."[b]

Paul certainly knows how to pour on the irony. Obviously, if you've done something sinful, selfish or questionable you can't come to the Father and give Him *thanks* for it. When you talk about doing things in Christ's name you are talking about *motives*. And when you talk about coming to God and giving Him thanks for what you've done or said you have an automatic check on your motives. Here is a practical way to evaluate what you have been doing (or what you are planning to do). As human beings we all have mixed motives. Coming to God constantly to give thanks for what we have been doing is a great way to sort these motives out.

The "perfect" Christian family, group, church, etc. is not completely attainable this side of the pearly gates, but that doesn't mean you can't make a few improvements right now. The place to start is with yourself. Sanctification is a matter of getting to know the Person of Christ better and better. As you know Him better you start seeing others as more than just "people." As you let the words of Christ enrich your life . . . as you seek to do all things in His name . . . you start seeing people as persons—with needs, problems, hang-ups, feelings—all the things that are part of your own experience.

TAKE A LOOK AT YOUR LIFE-STYLE

The Supernatural point of view . . .

Reread Paul's tremendous thoughts in Col. 3:10-17. Then compare this passage with what he says in Eph. 4:1-32 and Eph. 5:1-20. Write in your own words what you think Paul feels the Christian life is all about. What makes a Christian tick?

If you'd like to do some further reading . . .

Love Is Now, Pete Gillquist, Zondervan Publishing House, 1970, contains perceptive insights on what Paul is talking about in Col. 3:10-17.

Taste of New Wine, Keith Miller, Word Books, 1965, offers what might be called the Magna Carta of contemporary protest against lack of love, peace and other Christian virtues in today's churches. Miller is a seeker of reality and if you are seeking it he will strike a responsive chord in you.

Why Am I Afraid to Tell You Who I Am? John Powell, Peacock Books, Argus Communications, 1969, is one of the best and most readable books you can find on what is means to be a person and to deal with other persons.

Concerning people or persons . . .

No one can develop freely in the world and find a full life without feeling understood by at least one person. . . .—Dr. Paul Tournier.[4]

Most of us feel that others will not tolerate emotional honesty and communication. We would rather defend

141

our dishonesty on the grounds that it might hurt others; and, having rationalized our phoneyness into nobility, we settle for superficial relationships.
—John Powell [5]

Don't just sit there . . .

Get together with other Christians who are close to you and discuss honestly the state of "Christian community or fellowship" in your group, class, family or church. Measure your particular situation against the description in Col. 3:10-17. What might you do to improve matters? Be specific. Go over the "How to Have a Natural High" cartoon, p. 139 (also material on pp. 140-141) and brainstorm together on what you might do to build the "ideal Christian group."

Write your own prayer: "Lord, I want your Word to dwell in me and I want to do everything in your name, especially concerning (describe a situation you are facing).

CHAPTER 11

IS THIS CHRISTIAN
Love
BIT FOR
REAL OR
???

"Either this Christian love bit is for real, or it isn't."

That was the comment by veteran high school staff worker Gary Hess when he met with youth director Jim Griffin and high school coordinator Doug Carter to plan the 1970-71 winter camp for the La Crescenta (Calif.) Baptist Church High School Department.

With 1300 members in the church and over 200 students on the rolls in the High School Department, La Crescenta Baptist had plenty of *people* but Gary, Jim and Doug, and others on the staff were interested in doing more in-depth work with *persons*. They were interested in probing deeper into the meaning of Scriptures like Col. 3:14, "Let love guide your life, for then the whole church will stay together in perfect harmony."[b]

"As successful as things were in the department," recalls Hess, "we just didn't feel we were making it with the usual Sunday morning, Sunday evening, Wednesday night program. All of our kids weren't necessarily attending everything and forty-five minutes to maybe two hours maximum a week doesn't cut the mustard when you are involved practically twenty-four hours a day with the secular philosophy."

Working with Doug Carter's suggestion of "The Body of Christ," (from I Corinthians 12) the La Crescenta youth leaders promoted the 1970-71 winter camp with the theme SEVENTY-ONE—ONE WAY. Dates were set for December 30-January 2, and heavy emphasis was placed on camp being "a time of evaluating where you've been in your spiritual life and asking God to help you decide where you're going." As in previous winter camps held for La Crescenta Baptist youth, there would be no main speaker; instead, adult leaders would guide small discussion groups of around 15 members each.

Late on Wednesday afternoon a total of 98 campers and 13 counselors (including some 15 college freshmen) left for a spot called Canyon Meadows, located forty miles north of La Crescenta (a suburb of Los Angeles). At dinner that first night each camper received a slip of paper, on which was typed the name of part of the human body—for example, "tendon of the left leg" or "elbow of the right arm."

Using a huge crude drawing of a human form, youth director Jim Griffin then introduced the main theme of "the Christian Body," from I Corinthians 12. He explained this would be the unifying theme for the entire weekend. Seven discussion groups—each a main part of the body—would start meeting that evening: Left Arm, Right Arm, The Trunk, Left Leg, Right Leg, Left Foot, Right Foot. Christ, of course, would be the Head of the Body, in accordance with such Scripture as Eph. 1:22.

Of key importance was that each person in each main discussion group was assigned to represent a *specific body part*. Counselor Judy Hicks, who was "Fibula, Left Leg" recalls: "The Left Leg was incomplete without me. The Leg Muscles needed me. I needed the Tendons and so on. It all designated personal responsibility and worth. Every person at camp was a different part of the whole body. There were no repetitions. No one was superfluous."

The first of our carefully designed discussion sessions took place right after dinner with each group (Body part) meeting in a separate room. The setting was informal and everyone was equipped with dittoed discussion guides containing questions and Scripture references. A real effort was made to keep adult discussion leaders and students on the same level. Adults had no special surprise tactics or information to set them above other members of the Body.

To get things going in session 1, each camper was asked to "draw a picture" or graph of some kind illustrating his past spiritual experience. Each person was to go back over his life—his high points, low points, moments of breakthrough, moments of despair, and especially where he was at that moment on December 30, 1970. Everyone had opportunity to explain his drawing to the rest of the group and get a taste of "opening himself up" to fellow Christians.

Session 1 closed with "conversational prayer" and one girl pretty well summed things up for her group saying, "Lord, help us not to be afraid to be honest." Like many of her fellow campers she wanted to open herself up to those around her and understand them but she was fearful of letting others know and see her as she really was.

Thursday morning opened with breakfast and a devotional time based on I Corinthians 13. Campers were asked to take a half hour alone to read Paul's matchless passage on love and realize, "God loves me *this way*."

Session 2 opened at 9:30 that morning and the seven

parts of the Body grappled with questions out of I Corinthians 12 on how Christians can work together, why unity is hard to accomplish, what they could do about unity.

Highlight of session 2 for the Left Leg (discussion group led by Gary Hess and Judy Hicks) was an observation by Jeanette, a quiet, sensitive junior. She said:

"It's impossible to get to know all 100 people up here, and if I can't get to know and love 100 people up here, how can I get to know and love the whole Body back at church? Well, my fingers only come in contact with my feet once in a while, but when they do, they help them—for example, they put on my shoes. My fingers come in contact with my thumb *continually*, so there's a stronger relationship there."

"She gave us a beautiful truth," recalls Gary Hess. "When you make a contact with another part of the Body, make the most of it. Help that part in any way you can, but don't feel guilty if you can't know and love all parts of the Body fully all the time. Jeanette put our group at ease about not having to go out and make close friends with all 100 people in the camp in order to be 'in the whole Body.' We felt free to concentrate on getting to know one another in our own group."

After lunch on Thursday campers were free to play, walk, talk or participate in an informal rap session in the main lodge led by Jim Griffin.

The Body takes a trust walk

Following dinner Thursday night (New Year's Eve) all members were briefed on taking a "trust walk" in preparation for discussion group session 3. First they read Eph. 4:1-4, which talks about walking in a manner worthy of your calling, diligently preserving the unity of the Spirit because there is one Body and one Spirit.

For the trust walk, all campers were instructed to "pair up and allow another member of Christ's Body to lead you with your eyes closed for five minutes. We want you to experience trusting another person and then switch roles. Keep track of times you opened your eyes and why. Remember the feeling that caused you to lose your trust."

The trust walk was probably the high point of the camp for counselor Judy Hicks and she describes it this way:

"We met in our group's room and were told about the trust walk. It was dark outside and cold. The camp grounds were covered with rocky fields, low-hanging branches, ponds, puddles, and a stream ran right through the middle. The Left Leg paired off in twos. Coreen, who was the Kneecap of our group and I, the Fibula, went together and this emphasized again our relationship to one another.

"As I was led around I could hear other pairs of people passing us. The grounds were swarming with what would have been a puzzling sight to an uninformed observer: 50 timid, blind, hesitating, ungraceful humans being led by 50 eager-but-finding-it-difficult-to-empathize partners. I opened my eyes twice—both times my leader stopped too sharply and pulled me back. When we changed roles I led Coreen for a while by the arm, and then told her I would walk beside her to keep her from harm but would not hold her directly. Insecurity set in immediately. She slowed her pace by half. But as we talked she relaxed and grew more confident. The test of her faith in me was obviously greater when she had only my voice to follow, but the learning was greater also."

Later all parts of the Body got into their groups to

discuss I John 4:7-19, and their experiences on the trust walk. Two boys had gotten out on the football field and literally run together. Others had jumped off of huge rocks into the waiting arms of helpers below. Some had walked within a few feet of the edge of the creek running through camp (in some spots it was a 10-foot drop down a sheer bank to the rocks and water below), with nothing more than instructions from their guide to go so many steps to the left, so many steps to the right, etc. These and other experiences triggered a great deal of animated discussion on what it means to trust God and to trust brothers and sisters in Christ.

Session 3 ended for the Left Leg with everyone getting together in the center of the room, arms around each other somewhat in football huddle fashion, each person uttering a one-word prayer. Included were prayers like "thanks" . . . "warmth" . . . "health" . . . "peace" . . . "security" . . . "eternal" . . . "beautiful" "strength" . . . "love". . . .*

At 9:30 that evening all campers met in the main lodge for a "Body Meeting." As 1970 came to a close, they sang, shared what had gone on in their groups, what the past year had meant, what they hoped for the new one. There was no main speaker or major entertainment—just sharing among Christians who recognized themselves as the Body of Christ.

*One-word prayers were one of several devices and symbols used to teach unity in the Body of Christ during the camp. Another idea used by Gary Hess in his group was called "affirmation prayer." The entire Left Leg sat in a circle, legs extended towards the center, with feet touching. Everyone made certain he knew the name of the person opposite him and then he would pray for that person by name, thanking God for something positive about that person. At another point in the camp one part of the Body—the Left Arm—was tied to a tree ouside of the dining hall after lunch. All of them would have had to stay tied to the tree until dinner if someone hadn't released them. Their instructions were to give no one any reasons for why they were tied up. One boy finally came along and untied them. Many campers clearly saw the connection between being one in the Spirit and helping one another.

Communion was served just before midnight. The campers saw the New Year in, quietly thinking about themselves and Christ.

New Year's Day was pretty well spent in taking it easy. Campers watched bowl games, talked, played. Gary Hess recalls that, "The only thing that went wrong was that the counselors played the high school guys in football in the afternoon and I missed seeing Stanford beat Ohio State in the last half of the Rose Bowl!"

After dinner on New Year's night, all parts of the Body convened for the fourth and final group discussion session. They reflected on the past two days and the progress made in their groups. They talked about what had meant most to them, what had been relevant, how much unity and trust they had experienced. After reading from Heb. 10:11-25, they talked about how Jesus has helped all Christians and how Christians can help one another. One of the main goals in session 4 was to help people face up to possible attitudes of not caring and indifference, as well as sharing feelings of success and unity.

Many people felt the camp had peaked on New Year's Eve with the trust walk, discussion group and Communion at midnight. But SEVENTY-ONE—ONE WAY was to climax in an even more dramatic fashion on Saturday morning just before packing the bus to leave. Another Body meeting was held in the main lodge, significantly titled "Body Communion." All seven Body parts met in their discussion rooms briefly and then Gary Hess led each group—hands linked together —into the main lodge. First came the Torso, then the Left Arm and Right Arm, the Left Leg and Right Leg, and finally the Left Foot and Right Foot (see diagram next page).

Jim Griffin describes the Body Communion this way:

HOW THE BODY TOOK COMMUNION

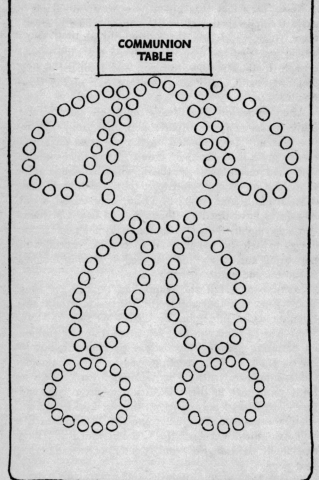

COMMUNION
TABLE

"All seven groups sat on the floor and we attached them together in a continuous shape like a huge body. Then I went around—sort of like a roll call—and asked, 'Is the Right Hand here?' and they raised their hands. Then I asked, 'Is the Left Arm here?' and so it went. No one had told the kids ahead of time they would be seated in the shape of a body but they caught on almost immediately. You could see the insight forming on their faces. They were saying to themselves, 'Hey, this IS the Body!'

"The Communion table was at the head. Counselors came forward for the elements and this helped keep the symbolism going. Nutrients were coming from the Head (meaning Christ), the counselors were acting as 'the bloodstream' taking the elements back to their respective parts of the Body. We all linked up by having each person put his right hand on the knee of the person next to him. That left everyone with only one hand free. We passed the bread in seven huge chunks—one chunk for each main Body part. One person would hold it while the other broke off a small piece. Then that person would hold it while the next person broke off a piece.

"We drank from seven cups using the same procedure. One person would drink, then hold the cup while the next person wiped the edge of the cup with a napkin. Then he would take the cup and drink and hold it while the next person wiped the cup, and so on. The whole idea was to have us linked together as one Body, dependent on one another and of one Spirit."

For Griffin, one of the more significant moments in the closing Body Communion came when he announced that there had been some breakage and other additional expenses for the weekend. There was no lengthy plea of any kind. One or two baskets were passed as the entire group stood to sing "How Great

151

Thou Art." A total of $47 was collected—almost 50 cents a camper—this, after each person had paid $27 each for the weekend. The entire group filed out singing "They'll Know We Are Christians by Our Love," which includes a line that had new significance for all of them—"We are one in the Spirit, we are one in the Lord!"

Nor did the impact of SEVENTY-ONE—ONE WAY end that morning. Many campers reached home still in a state of euphoric enthusiasm and a new feeling of oneness in Christ. They got the whole church excited, including senior pastor Bernard Travaille, who made the Body of Christ concept his topic for a series of three sermons and his stewardship theme for the next year. One service lasted 90 minutes, with 500 worshippers gripped by the same powerful feeling of being "one in the Spirit" that had prevailed at SEVENTY-ONE—ONE WAY.

About two weeks after camp, Jim Griffin and Judy Hicks compiled a brief evaluation questionnaire and asked a cross-section of young people who had attended SEVENTY-ONE—ONE WAY for some feedback.

Did the campers recognize the purpose, the organizers had in mind? Jeanette put it well when she said, "To make people feel they are individuals and each have their own function as a part of the entire Body of Christ."

"United as one . . ." "One in the Spirit . . ." "To unify the body . . ." were typical answers. The "One in Christ" idea had definitely gotten through.

Had campers' purposes changed while they were there? Some did, some didn't. Most dramatic perhaps was Steve, who went into camp a worshipper of Tarot cards and Satan and a user of certain ESP powers as a means of taking a personal ego trip. Counselor Ron Wertz, who led discussions in Steve's group, had several personal talks with him and Steve admitted his fear of the occult and his loneliness. He wrote on his questionnaire concerning his change of purpose: "You'd better believe it! In that I switched from Satanic worship to Jesus my sweet Lord. I did this because I was locked in a lonely and freaky cage with all the sin I wanted and I needed someone like Jesus to clear the air."

When campers were asked if their own personal purpose had been fulfilled, Carol responded: "Wow, yes. I can't think of a better way to start the New Year than taking Communion. I rededicated my life that night and *no way* am I going to lose my faith in Christ."

Perhaps the key question on the evaluation sheet was: "Do you still feel one in the Spirit? Why or why not?" In other words, can a mountaintop experience at camp carry over to the valley of daily routine back at school, jobs, family and in church itself?

Ken summed it up candidly when he said: "I do, but not as much as when I was at Canyon Meadows. I think the feeling isn't as strong because of the atmosphere. When I was at camp I was helped by other Christians but now school makes me feel not as spiritually strong."

Where do they all go?

Debbie reported: "Our group has continued meeting . . . but at home by myself I lose all thought really that there are others going through the same trials and joys I am. I need fellowship and Christian friends. Camping is great for that reason, but where do they all go when we get home?"

"Where they all go . . ." is a matter of real concern to Jim Griffin and other youth leaders in his church. Working with what he calls his "Five Year Plan," Griffin is continually developing and evaluating programs that will get La Crescenta Baptist young people together in as many creative, Bible-centered situations as possible. These include: winter and summer camps, a "now" kind of youth choir called the "Sounds of Purpose," Sunday morning Seminar classes, Wednesday night youth prayer meeting, and small groups meeting in homes during the week for Bible study and prayer.*

In this kind of overall program, Griffin sees the balance and variety needed to help young people mature in Christ. He bases his approach to Christian education on Acts 2:42,43: "They joined with the other believers in regular attendance at the apostles' teaching sessions and at the Communion services and prayer meetings. A deep sense of awe was on them all. . . ."b

"At the very center is learning," he says, "and then you go into fellowship and prayer. All this is done in the context of ministry. It's a *balanced diet*. I tell the kids that if they are out of balance on any of these things they are not walking with Jesus and they certainly aren't running with Him. They are dragging. You have to have this balanced diet with *all* the nutrients. This sytem fits hand in glove with the way we are constructed. If the center is the mind, then we have our emotions and then we have our volition or our will. You need a balanced diet if you want to grow."

Achieving this kind of balance is a constant challenge to Jim Griffin and those who work with him. It is one thing to point in the Scriptures to a verse such as Col. 1:18: "He is the Head of the body made up of His

*Sunday Morning Seminar replaced traditional Sunday School Classes at La Crescenta Baptist several years ago. Following SEVENTY-ONE—ONE WAY Jim Griffin was planning to expand the Seminar program and offer courses on Tuesday mornings before school and on Saturdays. He also hoped to develop "circles of concern," in which students would be organized according to geographical area and would meet together regularly in homes to study, pray and encourage one another.

people . . ."[b] but it is another to get Christians of any age to recognize what this means experientially *for them*. It is one thing to read about letting love guide your life and having the whole church stay together in perfect harmony (Col. 3:14[b]) and actually living that way even for a few days at camp. It is one thing to talk about the peace of heart which comes from Christ being present in the hearts and lives of members of His Body (Col. 3:15[b]) and actually experiencing that kind of peace in a meaningful way with other Christians.

This is why Jim Griffin especially treasures one bit of positive feedback on SEVENTY-ONE—ONE WAY—a comment that came from a teenager who is one of the leaders in the La Crescenta Baptist High School Department. When Dan returned from camp his father wondered what he'd say because in the past he had often been a bit pessimistic about "Mickey Mouse" Christian events and programs. "How was it?" the father asked.

"Just right!"

TAKE A LOOK AT YOUR LIFE-STYLE

The Supernatural point of view . . .

Paul's tremendous thoughts in Col. 3:10-17 are great theory, but Paul never stops with theory. In Col. 3:18-4:1 he gets down to the nitty-gritty of living out all of these Christian virtues and sanctified actions in the places where you can't fake it: the home and on the job. "On the job," by the way, includes school, working with teachers, administrators, students, etc. (It also includes teamwork, working with the coach, other players, etc.) The following is Col. 3:18-4:1 from *The Living Bible*. Read it through a couple of times and compare it carefully with Col. 3:10-17. Then take a few minutes to write down ideas for making Col. 3:10-

17 a reality in your own situation with your family, with employers, teachers, school administrators, wherever you are living out your Christian experience.

"You wives, submit yourselves to your husbands, for that is what the Lord has planned for you. And you husbands must be loving and kind to your wives and not bitter against them, nor harsh. You children must always obey your fathers and mothers, for that pleases the Lord. Fathers, don't scold your children so much that they become discouraged and quit trying. You slaves must always obey your earthly masters, not only trying to please them when they are watching you but all the time; obey them willingly because of your love for the Lord and because you want to please Him. Work hard and cheerfully at all you do, just as though you were working for the Lord and not merely for your masters, remembering that it is the Lord Christ who is going to pay you, giving you your full portion of all He owns. He is the one you are really working for. And if you don't do your best for Him, He will pay you in a way that you won't like—for He has no special favorites who can get away with shirking. You slave owners must be just and fair to all your slaves. Always remember that you, too, have a Master in heaven who is closely watching you."

If you'd like to do some further reading . . .

Groups in Action, by Lyman Coleman, The Halfway House, copyright, 1968 is one of many approaches to Bible study designed to produce Christian community and concern. If you are interested in starting your own small group, this is one way to get off the ground. Many of Coleman's ideas were used by the La Crescenta Baptist Church winter camp, SEVENTY-ONE—ONE WAY. He has a number of excellent Bible study packages available through *Serendipity Books*, Creative Resources, Word Publications, Waco, Texas.

Don't just sit there . . .

Go over the key ideas in Chapter 11 (see "One in the Spirit, One in the Lord" section of "Blueprint for a Christian Life-style," pp. 182-183). Think and pray about finding yourself a group or starting one. Jim Griffin points out that you only need one other person and a wholehearted commitment by you and that person to be honest and faithful. The rest is up to the Holy Spirit.

Write your prayer: "Lord, the idea of getting into a small group where there is honesty and openness about You is

CHAPTER 12

Why not PRAY about it for a change?

"God, this last year has been a glorious experience with You—we've shared so much! . . . each day we talk to one another. In my problems, You help me toward a solution. When I don't think I will make it through another day, I do."

"Yes, I guess prayer is important, but if I were honest I'd have to say I don't do it much."

"Oh, I admit, there are still those times when I am very confused and everything is cluttered up in my mind. But if I just close my eyes, take myself out of this world for an instant, you come through loud and clear . . ."

"Pray? Why? God has it all programmed doesn't he?"

"Father, I know I cannot spread Your Word as forcefully and effectively as some. But still You are working through me—and I am aware of it. I wish everyone could feel the peace that I have . . ."

"I've tried praying, but I never get any answers. I either don't know how, or I don't live right!"

According to comments like those above, the answer to "Why not pray about it?" depends on a person's point of view. For some, prayer is an absolute necessity for living in an unchristian world. Prayer is power. Prayer is positive. Prayer really works.[1]

Others, however, confess frustration, boredom, or "lack of answers." Some admit they see no reason to pray, or that they "know they should" but don't.

What makes the difference? Are some people psychologically geared to get something out of prayer while others are not? Is prayer really important? Is it worth the time? Is it "required duty" for all Christians?

Prayer problems aren't unique with twentieth century hang-ups and distractions. Paul had to deal with them in A.D. 62 and that's why he told the Colossians:

"Don't be weary in prayer; keep at it; watch for God's answers and remember to be thankful when they come. Don't forget to pray for us too, that God will give us many chances to preach the Good News of Christ for which I am here in jail. Pray that I will be bold enough to tell it freely and fully, and make it plain, as, of course, I should"[b] (Col. 4:2-4).

Pretty brief. Paul seems to need some help with his evangelistic work (and who wouldn't chained to a guard in a Roman prison?). But there doesn't seem to be a whole lot of specific help for the Christian who "knows prayer is important, but doesn't do it much."

Watch for God's answers? For some people it seems that lately He has been awfully heavy with "'wait awhile." As for praying in groups, *that* reminds them of attending a zombie convention. Without admitting it out loud or even to themselves, they drift into prayerlessness with the excuse: "Why bother to pray?"

Which is, of course, a perfect way to commit slow spiritual suicide. That's why Paul says, "Don't be weary

. . . stick with it." In other words, keep the communication lines open.

Prayer is, after all, conversation with God. It's better than a hot line, a two-way radio or even Telstar. Prayer is instant communication with God anytime, anywhere.

When Jesus "emptied Himself" (Phil. 2:5-11) and left heaven to live on earth as a man, He realized He needed the Father's strength. He always made it a point to get alone with God (Luke 5:16). He prayed for strength in Gethsemane to meet the final crisis on Golgotha (see Luke 22:41,42). His Lord's Prayer is a model used by millions (Matt. 6:9-13). His prayer for the Church in John 17 is perhaps the most beautiful ever uttered.

If the Son felt He had to communicate with His heavenly Father, how about the Christian living in the unchristian twentieth century? Was Jesus thinking about us when He said:

"Ask, and you will be given what you ask for. Seek, and you will find. Knock, and the door will be opened. For everyone who asks, receives. Anyone who seeks, finds. If only you will knock, the door will open"[b] (Matt. 7:7,8).

"Keep alert and pray. Otherwise temptation will overpower you. For the spirit indeed is willing, but how weak the body is"[b] (Matt. 26:41).

"You haven't tried this before, [but begin now]. Ask, using My name, and you will receive, and your cup of joy will overflow"[b] (John 16:24).

These words by Jesus should be enough to convince us that prayer isn't some sort of religious duty we had better do or else. Prayers are not spiritual nickels to put in a celestial vending machine. God wants us to talk to Him because He wants to help us, strengthen us, love us, know us.

Through prayer God gives you strength and power

—for living at home, at school, at work—wherever the daily routine takes you. Even when your prayers don't seem to be getting answered, just remember that God is at work within you. Paul found this out when he prayed three times for God to take away his "thorn in the flesh." God didn't take away the thorn but He did say this to Paul: "I am with you; that is all you need. My power shows up best in weak people." And Paul understood because his reply was: "I am quite happy about 'the thorn' . . . for when I am weak, then I am strong—the less I have, the more I depend on Him"* (see II Cor. 12:9, 10).

Do you need an appointment?

Most Christians would agree with all of this reasoning on the benefits of prayer. They know that God wants them to "keep in touch." But a lot of them don't seem to log much more time in prayer. Do they think they need an appointment?

Jesus didn't seem to need any appointments. He often prayed alone (Mark 1:32-35; Luke 6:12,13). He told his disciples, "When you pray, go away by yourself, all alone, and shut the door behind you and pray to your Father secretly, and your Father, who knows your secrets, will reward you"* (Matt. 6:6).

Of course we know intuitively praying alone makes sense. There are some things you want to talk over with God in private . . . sins to confess . . . dreams and ambitions you don't want to share with others. Then, too, talking it over with God often makes it possible to talk over a difficult situation with another person or persons.

And one thing about God—He will not talk you to death. He will not force you to share with Him in prayer. Instead He waits and draws you, until you finally respond. When you are ready, He is ready. He always has been and always will be.

In her excellent book, *Prayer: Conversing with God,* Miss Rinker lists some practical pointers[2] for making private prayer a part of daily life:

1. Pick your spot where you can pray alone. Maybe it's a chair, an unused room, a desk or even in your car. But have a place where you can go.

2. Look forward to your time of prayer as you would an appointment with an important person. Tell yourself you are going to meet with God, that you are going to be together. He's going to show you Himself. You are going to put aside all else and worship Him.

3. Try praying aloud or at least in semiaudible tones. Miss Rinker points out that praying aloud helps you remember you are praying to someone else and hearing your own voice keeps your thoughts centered on God.

4. Use daily devotional books or Bible study materials. (See p. 169 for ideas.)

But suppose you still have trouble finding that quiet spot or you still don't seem to be able to keep your mind on what you want to say. One girl's solution for this was writing her prayers on paper. Cindy Randolph became a Christian while in college and found that her dorm was too noisy for doing much concentrating. She reports in *Decision* magazine that she ". . . either had to pray on paper or in the tub with the water running —and there's a limit to the number of baths one can take!" Here are some of Cindy's prayers, printed in her personal "lowercase" style:

dear jesus

my life started august 8, 1969. what a fool i was not to learn of you sooner! seventeen years have been wasted— but i guess you have a time and a place for everything. you planned it this way, didn't you? thanks for not letting me waste any more time.

thanks for a wonderful day. thank you for my christian friends and thank you for my not-so-christian friends—just thanks for everything.

i just realized something fantastic. wherever i am, i am never alone. never am i to be alone again. i have you and you have me.

it's hard for a person with my reputation to go back and try to be a christian. people at school still expect me to be a hell-raiser. please don't let me fall. don't leave me when it's the roughest. i love you and need you so.

what do you want to do with my life? you know, sometimes i'd like to crawl behind your eyes and see me the way you see me. sometimes i get so self-centered i can't see past my own nose.

you know, it's really great to have someone like you who really listens to my problems and helps me to learn how to handle them. with you and me working together we could be quite a team! thank you for lighting the candle in my heart. love cindy[a]

Whether you pray on paper as Cindy Randolph did; whether you pray semiaudibly as Rosalind Rinker suggests; or whether you simply find a quiet place and pray silently to God alone, praying secretly doesn't sound too threatening. After all, if you stumble and grope for words, God understands. In fact we are guaranteed from Scripture that even when we can't think of what to say, ". . . the Holy Spirit prays for us with such feeling that it cannot be expressed in words. And the Father who knows all hearts knows, of course, what the Spirit is saying as He pleads for us in harmony with God's own will"[b] (Rom. 8:26,27).

It's true Jesus said we should go into our closets and pray, but He also said: "Where two or three gather together because they are Mine, I will be right there among them'" (Matt. 18:20). Rosalind Rinker, who has written several practical and relevant books on prayer (see titles, p. 169), testifies that she has experienced Christ's presence while praying with others again and again and so can anyone else. Before she learned the secret of praying with others she thought her burdens were greater than anyone else's. "Now I know they aren't," she says, "and now I know a way to help instead of always wanting to be helped."[4]

Conversational prayer: dialogue with God and others

Rosalind Rinker calls her "way to help" *conversational* prayer. When you are in a real conversation you are aware of others, their rights, privileges and feelings. If you talk to them long enough you are aware of their total personality.

A good conversation is one in which the participants take turns. A monologue with one person doing all the talking and the other nodding in polite boredom is not a conversation. As you converse you should stick to the subject and exchange ideas on that subject. In a significant, interesting conversation every participant makes full use of his memory, his patience, his alertness, his manners. In a real conversation everyone is *tuned in*.

So how does all this apply to prayer? Rosalind Rinker recalls a true incident in which she taught conversational prayer to a group of college students. They were about to follow their usual procedure of "praying around the circle" until everyone had had his usual chance, when she tactfully suggested that there might be another way to let the Holy Spirit guide more specifically and effectively. The group was eager to learn and she pointed out that the first thing to remember is that the Lord Jesus is right there in the center of any

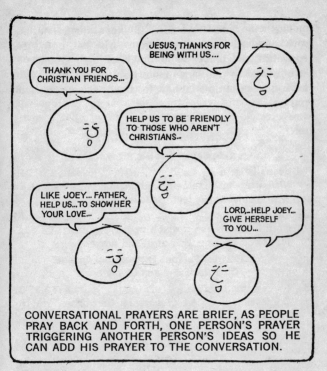

CONVERSATIONAL PRAYERS ARE BRIEF, AS PEOPLE PRAY BACK AND FORTH, ONE PERSON'S PRAYER TRIGGERING ANOTHER PERSON'S IDEAS SO HE CAN ADD HIS PRAYER TO THE CONVERSATION.

circle. Each person should talk directly to Him. When he's talking about himself, use the pronoun "I." When he is speaking for the whole group he should use "We."

She also stressed praying by subjects. If someone prays for a certain person others can pray for him too. Directness and simplicity is the key. The Holy Spirit guides as the whole group stays on one subject at a time and several people might pray about that subject, person, problem, etc. Prayers are brief and people pray back and forth, one person's prayer triggering another person's ideas so he can add his prayer to the conversation.

The collegians tried Miss Rinker's suggestion and revolutionized their prayer group. She has introduced conversational prayer to hundreds of such groups personally and to thousands more through her books. Following is her outline on how to engage in conversational prayer.

CONVERSATIONAL PRAYER
We Begin with His Presence

1. Jesus Is Here . . . . Matt. 18:19,20
   Visualize Him. Use creative imagination. Be silent. Be a little child at His feet. He loves you.

2. Thank You, Lord . . . . Phil. 4:4-7
   Gratitude is worship which opens the heart. Be audible, brief, specific. Use open-end prayer.

We Pray for Persons Present and Absent
Thus Receiving and Giving Love

3. Forgive me, Lord . . . . James 5:13-16
   Confession is a part of worship. Be honest. Pray for yourself, then others will pray for you.
   This is prayer response.
   Say "I" when you mean yourself.
   Say "we" when all present can be included.

4. Help my brother . . . . Mark 11:22-25
   Prayer-response should be audible, brief, with love and thanksgiving. Use first names. The Holy Spirit will give you words when you pray. Give thanks when someone prays for you.
   This is agreeing in prayer.

This Is Love in Action

Love one another as I have loved you . . . . John 15:12
Ask whatever you will and it shall be done . . John 15:7

This prayer from the heart is love in action. We become involved in God's purposes, in His viewpoint, and with each other's needs. Then the circle will widen to include family, friends, nation, the world.[5]

Still not sure about how it all works? The following comes from *Prayer: Conversing with God*—an actual prayer conversation among five teenagers:

"Sue: Jesus, thanks for being with us tonight.

Bev: It's great to have friends, Lord. Thank You for these Christian friends You have given me.

Sue: But Lord, help us to be friends to our buddies at school who aren't Christians.

Katie: Like Joey . . . Father, help us . . . to show her that real happiness comes as we serve You.

Bev: Help her to see that it is not boring to be a Christian.

Sue: Lord . . . help Joey to give herself to You . . .

Muriel: And thanks, Lord Jesus, for . . ."⁶

Tips on praying conversationally

Some things to remember about conversational prayer:

1. You can go on as long as you want to.

2. You can make up requests as you go along. Instead of "talking about what you're going to pray about," just start praying.

3. You can actually stop right in the middle of your prayer time and tell the group something if you remember it. This is what is known as *relaxed* conversational prayer. You can agree with someone else's prayer or add on to it. This is what Matthew 18:19,20 is talking about. Jesus wants Christians to agree in prayer!⁷

In their contemporary Christian youth musical, *Show Me!* Jimmy and Carol Owens include the song "Long Distance Love." One stanza in the song (sung by Joey and Julie, two young people searching for spiritual reality) goes like this:

"This God you listen to . . .

The One with all the plans and new directions,
How does He talk to you?
How does He find a way to make connections?

Does He distribute tracts or does He buy some time on
local radio,
Or does He come to you and tell you like a friend the
things you need to know?"

The song's refrain says:

"Long distance love is not for me; I need communication.
I need a friend that I can see; I need the warm vibration,
that is real love, that is real love."⁸

In *Show Me!* these are the words of non-Christians
who are searching for God. But a lot of their ideas
could apply just as well to Christians who sometimes
feel that God's love comes to them long distance and
that they are lacking in warm vibrations.

If your Christian life is lacking those "good vibes,"
why not take the suggestions in this chapter, get off by
yourself or with some friends and pray about it (for a
change)?

TAKE A LOOK AT YOUR LIFE-STYLE
The Supernatural point of view . . .

Why pray? One good reason: God tells you to. See I
Chron. 16:11, Matt. 7:7; 26:41, Luke 18:1, John
16:24, Eph. 6:18, Phil. 4:6, I Thess. 5:17.

Why pray? Because it's a way to "get in touch with
God." See Deut. 4:29, Ps. 105:4, Isa. 55:6, Acts 17:27.

Why pray? Because God has promised to answer.
See Ps. 91:15, Isa. 58:9; 65:24, John 15:7. You say
your prayers are "bouncing off the ceiling"? There are
causes for failure in prayer. They include disobedience

(I Sam. 28:1-19); secret sin (Ps. 66:18); indifference (Prov. 1:28,29); instability and doubt (James 1:6,7); selfishness (James 4:3).

So how do you learn to pray successfully? You need to feel repentance and contrition (in other words be truly sorry for what you have fouled up in life). See II Chron. 7:14. You should be sincere (Jer. 29:13). You need faith and trust (Mark 11:24). You need righteousness and obedience, which comes only through trusting in Christ (James 5:16, I John 3:22).

Above all you should keep on praying as Christ taught in Luke 11:5-13.

If you'd like to do some further reading . . .

Rosalind Rinker's outstanding books on prayer provided many of the ideas for this chapter. They include: *Prayer: Conversing with God,* Zondervan, 1959; *Communicating Love Through Prayer,* Zondervan, 1966; *Teaching Conversational Prayer,* Word Books, 1970.

For helps on prayer and the devotional life:

Praying: How to Start and Keep Going, Bobb Biehl and James W. Hagelganz, Regal Books, 1977.

Devotional Thoughts for Youth, Walter L. Cook, Abingdon Press, 1975.

Going Steady with God, Anna Mow, Zondervan, 1972.

Concerning prayer . . .

"Prayer is the expression of the human heart and conversation with God. The more natural the prayer, the more real He becomes. It has all been simplified for me to this extent: Prayer is a dialogue between two persons who love each other."—Rosalind Rinker[9]

Don't just sit there . . .

Go over the practical suggestions in this chapter and start doing something about improving your prayer life —private or public. Take "prayer inventory":

1. Do I have a private place to pray? If so, how often do I use it?

2. Do I look forward to praying as I do to meeting with a special friend?

3. Have I tried praying semiaudibly or in writing in order to keep my mind on talking to God?

4. Do I have any kind of daily devotional book to give me ideas on how to pray more creatively to give me a fresh slant on talking to God?

5. Am I willing to put myself out to pray with others?

6. Have I tried conversational prayer or am I willing to do so?

Write your own prayer.
"Lord, about prayer, I just want to say

Being a Christian then, is...

Paul is almost through with his blueprint for being a Christian in an unchristian world. He seems to be hurrying as he tucks in a few reminders about spreading the Gospel—almost as an afterthought:

"Make the most of your chances to tell others the Good News. Be wise in all your contacts with them. Let your conversation be gracious as well as sensible, for then you will have the right answer for everyone"[b] (Col. 4:5,6).

Brief as Paul's words on witnessing are, they contain a concise but complete statement of how to get out the Good News—whether it's the first century or the twentieth: be ready, be wise, be right. Paul wanted the Colossians to always be ready to share their feelings, experience and knowledge of Christ with others. He also wanted them to be wise--to use timing and tact in their witness for Christ. The same holds true for Christians in today's unchristian world. Admittedly, it isn't always easy. One person's idea of what is winsome, winning and witty is somebody else's idea of gross, gauche and gruesome.

Perhaps above all Paul wanted the Colossians and all Christians to be *right*. He wrote his letter to Colosse to make sure they didn't get the Good News confused with a lot of pseudophilosophical drivel. He spent a lot of time telling the Colossians (and us) what we have in Christ and who Christ really is.

Paul knew that if you have things straight about Christ, the source of truth, you are also plugged in to the source of power for being wise, gracious and sensible. And then you can work out your own strategy for reaching an unchristian world that is hurting . . . bad.

In his prose poem "Looking into a Decade" evangelist Larry Walker puts the whole thing in perspective:

SIGHTS AND SOUNDS OF THE SEVENTIES

Upward

Twin Towers 110 stories high

362 pasengers in a 747

Space satellite laboratories; the Moon, Mars and

Downward

A rat chewing on a baby's arm

A derelict stupored on a snowy sidewalk
    under a stolen coat

A main-lined needle speaking a vow
    that can scarcely be broken

Outward

How many millions starving in India?—
    'Oh, just Calcutta'?

172

Sounds like a play—or maybe only a broken record

Same song; different words; Bangkok, Biafra, Brooklyn

Inward

Crowded strap-hangers and city canyons,
  yet lonely emptiness

A noisy tube-box companion, yet restless,
  searching discontent

Stock portfolio, insurance, bank accounts, yet why
  such eternal insecurity?

Around the Corner

Hey, boy, in your place—get the pigs!

Beans, left-over borrowed bread—an inch-thick,
  medium rare

War: the defense of my right to say
  'My son was killed over there'

Next Door

What's their name? Don't forget the Christmas card.

Did you return the rake and hoe from last summer?

What's that? Gee, too bad. We really must send
  flowers.

All Over

It's either pagan Christianity or Christian paganism

Everything's redundant or at least repetitious

And self perpetuating—society tends to breed itself.

ISN'T THERE ANYONE WHO CARES?

Onward

THE Great Hope—There is Someone

Who cares . . . . AND can enable

Us to care for 'those'; even about ourselves

Forward

The pendulum of discouragement has swung backward
  far enough

It seems so dramatic to describe the debris

But we really better concentrate on HIM.[1]

And this is where Paul came in with his letter to Colosse, which also seems quite appropriate for any secular city or town of the 1970s. Like the first century Christian, the twentieth century believer would like to know what being a Christian in an unchristian world is all about. He would like to make some sense out of the most confusing scene of all time: jets, rockets, computers, the tube, Superbowl, cinema, Viet-Nam, Mei Lai, Manson's madness, drugs, trips, revolution, pornography, the Pentagon papers and pollution. If you try to fit Christianity into all that surrounds you it doesn't work. Christ doesn't fit into the unchristian world. The world and its problems are absorbed by Jesus Christ.

Being a Christian is no trip, no flight from reality, no panacea. There is really no special formula, no groovy new approach.

Being a Christian is what it always has been and always will be: believing, trusting and living in Christ—accepting the fact that this unknown carpenter from some camel stop called Nazareth was really more than a man—that He was God, actually, *God in the flesh*, and that He died for everyone's sins and rose from the dead.

They call this the Gospel, the Good News. And somehow, as improbable as it all sounds, the Gospel answers life's big questions. There is a God, He cares, and above all He forgives us for our very poor marksmanship. It isn't simply that we have missed the mark of knowing how to live. We haven't even been aiming in the right direction.

Being a Christian is experiencing a change of that direction as the Holy Spirit convicts you of your own sin (poor aim) and proceeds to "guide you into all truth . . ."[b] (John 16:13). As the earlier chapters of this book tried to point out, all truth is God's truth. According to Paul's entire train of thought in Colossians, Christianity is not a philosophy in competition with other philosophies. All philosophies—naturalism, rationalism, existentialism, etc.—live and move and have their being within God—Christ Himself. Theologian Addison Leitch puts it well when he says:

What other ground for truth can there be except in Truth Himself? It follows, then, does it not, that the work of the Holy Spirit could be manifested in many areas not usually thought of as religious or churchy. William Temple once remarked that on the day of judgment many good people will be surprised to discover that God is interested in many other subjects besides religion. God is surely interested in earthworms and oysters, the stars in their courses and the laughter of children. And if all truth is God's truth, then good Christian people should rejoice in mathematics and poetry, a nice double play, and statues in the park. In religious circles there has been a constant error, a false dichotomy, concerning the sacred and the secular. The Incarnation should have headed that off long ago; surely the idea of 'all truth' in the work of the Holy Spirit forces us to rethink such things.[2]

Interwoven with the Spirit's task of guiding the Christian into all truth is His primary goal of revealing Christ. "He shall glorify Me; for He shall take of Mine, and shall disclose it to you"[a] (John 16:14).

"Whatever is truly of the Spirit," says Addison Leitch, "will lead us to Christ. We recognize how this works out in experience. We set ourselves to examine the Spirit only to find that the longer we look at Him the more we are looking at Christ. This is a strange and also informative experience: Examine the Spirit and He is always pointing away from himself to Christ, so in a sense we miss the Spirit and find Christ. But this is the way it's supposed to be, this is the way the Trinity seems to function: We look at the Spirit and see Christ, who reveals the Father."[3]

All of which may suggest there is no one distinctive Christian life-style for the unchristian world of the twentieth century. For some people the Spirit works quietly, calmly; with others He erupts like a Yamaha 360 in a motorcross run. In any case the true work of the Holy Spirit of Christ is in building the Body of Christ. There are many life-styles but *only one Body*. Somehow Jesus Christ absorbs us all. Are you young, old or in-between? Are you establishment, counterculture or one of the silent majority who isn't sure which?

It doesn't matter. There is one Lord and one Faith—one Truth. This is what Paul has said again and again in his letter to the Colossians. Christ "was before all else began and it is His power that holds everything together"[b] (Col. 1:17).

The name of the game is Jesus Christ

It isn't just a matter of Jesus being right and everyone else being wrong. It's not that kind of ball game. The name of this game is Jesus Christ. All truth finds its verification and purpose in Jesus Christ who is final Truth.

The key to Christianity is that Jesus Christ really is the reason for it all and that He is holding it all together. He isn't *just* a sweet Lord who teaches tolerance and love. He isn't *just* a superstar who got murdered by the establishment. He is, in fact "the exact likeness of the unseen God . . . [because] . . . God wanted all of Himself to be in His Son"[b] (Col. 1:15,19).

Christ is indeed the great hope—actually *the only hope*. Society's debris is dramatic, depressing and disturbing. Opportunities for good or for evil are unlimited. The Second Coming may or may not be just around the corner. There are many prophets with theories and many theorists trying to sound like prophets. But being a Christian in the unchristian world is just what Paul has tried to tell you in the book of Colossians. You better concentrate on HIM.

Go Beyond Legalistic Games
(Chapter 7—Col. 2:16-23)

Religious legalism snares all of us, at one time or another, in games like: WISH I WERE A BETTER CHRISTIAN, GOOD CHRISTIANS DON'T, and GET ON THE BALL . . .

If you want to go beyond games to intimacy with Christ—share your life with Him—ask yourself these questions:

1. *Have I experienced the difference between going through religious motions and the Real Thing? Have I repented—turned from sin—and placed my faith in a sovereign, merciful God or have I decided to make Christ my cosmic buddy?*

2. *Do I really believe that in Christ I don't have a past—only a future? Are my sins all nailed to the cross, or do I still carry some of them? Do I look ahead to becoming what God wants me to be, or do I look back, not sure I really "belong"?*

3. *Do I know how to avoid being trapped into playing spiritual games? Do I realize I do not have the power to keep any decision, no matter how "noble" or "spiritual" it is? Do I live in the awareness that I am ALWAYS dependent on God?*

4. *Do I know Jesus personally or casually? Is He my intimate friend or a "religious acquaintance" to whom I go when in trouble or in need of advice on what to do? Do I really want to trust Jesus—be open and honest with Him?*

5. *Is my Christian life a case of "I must" or "I want"? Do I obey God, serve God, worship God because I am afraid to do otherwise or do I obey God because I love Him and want to obey Him?*

178

To sum it up: A Christian life-style does not start with you and what people advertise as God's rules. It starts with you and Jesus Christ. The "good life" lies in Him.

WHY PLAY GAMES WHEN YOU
CAN DO THE REAL THING?

Get on Target and Stay There . . .
(Chapter 8—Col. 3:1-4)

"Becoming sanctified" has its mystical side but it also involves practical everyday things any Christian can do in order to make Christ his real goal in living. Things you can do—right now—to get on target and stay there:

1. Stop playing GUESS I'LL NEVER BE SPIRITUAL ENOUGH. There are more positive things to do, such as . . .

2. Start each day with God's promises. If a good breakfast in your stomach is important, what about programming your computer (mind) with positive, strengthening Biblical ideas? Review sample list on p. 109.

3. Keep yourself going with God's pep talks. Use the principles of psycho-cybernetics to keep yourself "on target." Through God's Word the Holy Spirit can talk you out of failure, defeat and depression and give you success, victory and joy.

4. Practice selective computer programming. Being selective about what you see, hear, think about doesn't mean you run a 24-hour censoring bureau. But Phil. 4:8 makes good sense. Also, review the "taste test" on p. 112. Maybe you need better taste.

5. Always keep on praying . . . for it . . . because of it . . . about it . . .through it . . . around it . . . in spite of it.

6. Stay on target to take off the pressure. Making Christ your goal doesn't turn you into a religious kook; He enables you to get it all together, keep it all together and work it all out.

To sum it up: Heaven can't wait. Without a target you're aiming at nothing and sure to hit it. Letting heaven fill your thoughts is to let Christ fill your life. What are you waiting for?

MAKE JESUS YOUR TARGET AND YOU CAN'T MISS

Be a Thermostat, Not a Thermometer . . .
(Chapter 9—Col. 3:5-9)

It's true there are no pat answers to a lot of sticky ethical and moral situations. If you're ready for *Christian* ethics, every ethical decision you make includes the following questions:

1. *Am I being a thermometer or a thermostat? Does my environment (those around me) make me do what I do? Or, do I have enough Christian conviction and concern to try and change things, to create ethical and moral conditions instead of letting immoral standards of behavior influence me?*

2. *What is the fair and loving thing to do in the situation? Am I really interested in fair play? For whom?*

3. *What is my duty—moral obligation? Am I aware of the powerful drives toward self-interest that work within me? Do I take sin seriously or do I think "I can handle it"?*

4. *What do the Scriptures teach—in general or particular— concerning this situation? Do I think I can obey "the law of love" (to love God and neighbor—Matt. 22:37-39) without taking other Biblical laws and absolutes into account?*

5. *Which choice in the situation will strengthen my relationship to Christ: which choice will weaken it? Do I want to live close enough to Christ to let Him control all of my decisions, big or little?*

To sum it up: If you are interested in being a thermostat in a world choking on thermometers, the Holy Spirit will give you the energy to operate. He'll take you beyond mere wishful thinking about love and fair play. He will give you the desire to be fair and loving and the power to do it!
IT'S NOT WHAT PEOPLE THINK, BUT WHAT YOU ARE

Love One Another as He Loves You . . .
(Chapter 10—Col. 3:10-17)

Christian virtues can be tyrants if you make them "required religious duties." It's more practical to see unity, mercy, kindness, humility, meekness, patience, forgiveness, love and peace as goals and then follow Paul's suggestions for reaching those goals:

1. *"Remember what Christ taught and let His words enrich your lives and make you wise . . ."*[b] *(Col. 3:16). This doesn't mean memorizing verses from the Gospels, it means sharing your life with Christ, and letting Him share with you—the intimacy He referred to in John 15:1-7.*

2. *" . . . teach them (Christ's words) to each other and sing them out in psalms and hymns and spiritual songs, singing to the Lord with thankful hearts"*[b] *(Col. 3:16). Christians are told that only certain people have "the gift of teaching" the Word of God, but in one way all Christians teach (and learn from) one another.*

3. *"And whatever you do or say, let it be as a representative of the Lord Jesus . . ."*[b] *(Col. 3:17). Rule books covering every situation in life are unavailable or ineffectual. But this verse is a mini-handbook—really a standard for every and any situation.*

4. *". . . and come with Him into the presence of God the Father to give Him your thanks"*[b] *(Col.3:17), which is the perfect test for mixed motives. You can't give God thanks for the questionable, the phony, the plastic.*

To sum it up: As you know Christ better, Christian virtues become more and more a part of your personality and life-style.

THERE ARE NO PERFECT PEOPLE
ONLY PERSONS, WITH NEEDS

One in the Spirit, One in the Lord
(Chapter 11—Col. 3:15—4:1)

SEVENTY-ONE—ONE WAY, the winter camp held by La Crescenta Baptist Church High School Department, was an outstanding experience in Christian unity and helping everyone feel part of the Body of Christ. You may or may not ever get to participate in a camp like this, but there are principles to extract from SEVENTY-ONE—ONE WAY that you can use anywhere, anytime:

1. *Recognize the need for Christian community—genuine fellowship where people are sharing Christ, the Bible, and themselves with one another.*

2. *Commit yourself to an attitude of open-mindedness. Try*

to create an environment where this honesty and openness can be brought out.

3. *Be willing to submit to Scriptural demands and absolutes. Either Christ and the Bible are important (and that means authoritative) or they aren't. Don't fake it.*

4. *Reach out within your own sphere of influence. Be willing to involve yourself and give yourself to others. (There is no better place to try to do this than in your own family. Family life is a daily laboratory for experiential Christian living.)*

5. *Find yourself a group or start one. You only need one other person but you may be able to find several who are interested in grappling together about how Christianity can equip and strengthen a person for the pressures of daily living in an unchristian, secular world that is changing at an incredible pace.*

To sum it up: Christianity is something to be shared and the place to begin sharing it is right in your own family, group, class or church.

EITHER THIS CHRISTIAN LOVE BIT IS FOR REAL,
OR IT ISN'T

Communicate with God—Constantly . . .
(Chapter 12—Col. 4:2-4)

For the Christian, to say "Why pray?" is equal to asking, "Why breathe?" Remember:

1. *Prayer is important. If Jesus thought so, every Christian should.*

2. *Prayer isn't a duty, it is a necessity of life for the Christian.*

3. *Prayer does change things—especially you. Private prayer should be part of every Christian's experience. Jesus instructed all Christians to go into a quiet private spot to talk with God.*

4. *Private prayer is easier than praying with a group but Jesus also tells us to pray together, because of the strength and insight it can give us. One solution to "zombielike prayer meetings" is conversational prayer (see p. 166 to review outline).*

182

5. *Long distance love is not very satisfying. All of us want to feel close to the ones we love. We want to feel communication—"good vibrations." This certainly goes for Christians who want to feel and know God's love.*

To sum it up: As Cindy Randolph says in her prayer on p. 163: It's really great to have someone like God who really listens to your problems and helps you learn how to handle them. You and God—*working together*—can really be quite a team!

PRAYER IS THE FRESH AIR FOR CHRISTIAN LIVING
SO WHY HOLD YOUR BREATH?

Make the Most of It . . .
(Conclusion—Col. 4:5,6)

Paul wrote his letter to the Colossians to make sure they understood the Good News and how to share it. According to Paul's suggestions in Col. 4:5,6:

1. *Be ready to share the Good News and be wise in how you do that sharing. Tactfulness and wisdom aren't gimmicks you can turn on at just the right time. You need to be in constant touch with the One whom the Good News is all about.*

2. *Be right . . . about who Christ really is. The overpowering message in Colossians is that Christ is The Truth. You don't fit Christ into the incredible kaleidoscope of world problems and hang-ups. The world and its problems are absorbed by Jesus Christ.*

3. *Becoming a Christian is experiencing a change of direction in your life through the convicting power of the Holy Spirit.*

4. *Being a Christian is knowing the guidance and filling of the Holy Spirit.*

5. *The Holy Spirit works in different people in different ways. There are many Christian life-styles but only one Body, and Jesus Christ absorbs us all. He is the reason for it all and He is holding it all together. He is the only hope. Therefore, to sum it ALL up:*

CHRIST IS THE ANSWER
CONCENTRATE ON HIM

Resources and Bibliography

CHAPTER 1

1. C. S. Lewis, *Miracles* (New York: Macmillan, 1963), p. 11.
2. Adapted from *Death in the City,* Francis Schaeffer (Downers Grove, Ill.: Inter-Varsity Press, 1969), pp. 128-130.
3. Lewis, *Miracles,* p. 14.
4. Paul Edwards, ed., *Why I Am Not a Christian* (New York: Simon and Schuster, Copyright 1957 by George Allen and Unwin Ltd.), p. 50.
5. Anecdote on Vicki Stevens adapted from her article, "Pieces of the Puzzle," *Decision* magazine, August 1969, p. 3.
6. Lewis, *Miracles,* p. 36.

CHAPTER 2

1. Quoted in the article, "Sons of Thunder," by Ken Anderson. Reprinted by permission from *Christian Life* magazine. Copyright March 1970, Christian Life Publications, Inc., Gundersen Drive and Schmale Road, Wheaton, Illinois 60187, p. 42.
2. "Christ the Preeminent," Part 2 of a study of Colossians, *Eternity,* January 1964, p. 13.
3. See *Expository Dictionary of New Testament Words,* W. E. Vine (Old Tappan, N.J.: Revell, 1940), vol. III, p. 260.
4. C. S. Lewis, *God in the Dock* (Grand Rapids, Eerdmans Publishing Company, 1970) pp. 157, 158.
5. John Stott, *Basic Christianity.* Copyright Inter-Varsity Press, London. Used by permission of Inter-Varsity Press, Downers Grove, Illinois 60515, p. 20.
6. Thomas Carlyle, nineteenth century historian and philosopher.

CHAPTER 3

1. Adapted from the article, "Cut Loose," by Stanley Rock. Reprinted by permission from *His,* student magazine of Inter-Varsity Christian Fellowship. Copyright October 1962, pp. 1-3.
2. From *How to Give Away Your Faith,* by Paul Little. Copyright 1966 by Inter-Varsity Christian Fellowship. Used by permission of Inter-Varsity Press, Downers Grove, Illinois 60515, p. 81.
3. Little, *How to Give Away Your Faith,* p. 81.

CHAPTER 4

1. *UCSB Daily Nexus,* University of California at Santa Barbara daily newspaper.

2. Kenneth Kantzer, "Christ and the Scripture," *HIS* magazine, January 1966, p. 16.

3. "The Evangelical View of Authority," Chapel address by John R. W. Stott, reprinted in the bulletin of Wheaton College, February 1968, p. 5.

4. "The Evangelical View of Authority," Chapel address by John R. W. Stott.

5. Edward John Carnell, *An Introduction to Christian Apologetics* (Grand Rapids, Eerdman's Publishing Company, 1948), p. 201.

6. Rob Witmer, Wheaton College, quoted from "The Ultimate Answer," *Collegiate Challenge*, Vol. 9, No. 2, copyright 1970, p. 16.

7. Kantzer, "Christ and the Scripture," p. 17.

8. John R. W. Stott, *Christ the Controversialist* (Downers Grove, Ill.: Inter-Varsity Press, 1970), p. 90.

CHAPTER 5

1. See *The Letters to the Philippians, Colossians and Thessalonians,* translated and interpreted by William Barclay. Published by the Saint Andrew Press, Edinburgh, 1957 and in the U.S.A. by the Westminster Press, 1958, pp. 161-163.

2. Nancy Anthony, Wisconsin State University, quoted from "Voices of Joy," *Collegiate Challenge*, Winter, 1971; vol. 10, no. 1, pp. 9,10.

CHAPTER 6

1. Robert Hilburn, "Janis Joplin's Lifetime: A Rush," *Los Angeles Times,* October 7, 1970.

2. *The Journals of Soren Kierkegaard,* selected, edited and translated by Alexander Dru (Brooklyn: Fontana, 1958).

3. *No Exit,* Jean-Paul Sartre, quoted from the paperback compilation of *No Exit and Three Other Plays* (New York: Vintage Books, published by Alfred A. Knopf, Inc., and Random House, Inc. Copyright 1946 by Steward Gilbert; also, copyright 1948, 1949 by Alfred A. Knopf, Inc.), pp. 46,47. Quoted also in the article, "Sartre versus Christ" by Arthur Holmes, *HIS* magazine, March 1967. Mr. Holmes' article was a valuable resource for this chapter.

4. David Knighton, "Beyond Camus," *Decision* magazine, December 1970, p. 5.

5. Knighton, "Beyond Camus," p. 5.

6. Robert Crossley, *We Want to Live* (Downers Grove, Ill.: Inter-Varsity Press, 1967).

CHAPTER 7

1. Patti Bard and Judi Culbertson, *Games Christians Play* (New York: Harper & Row, 1967). Sections of the book appeared earlier in somewhat different form in the May 1966 issue of *Eternity* magazine.
2. Eric Berne, *Games People Play* (New York: Grove Press, Inc., 1967), paperback edition, p. 18.
3. See *Games People Play*, pp. 115, 116.
4. Berne, *Games People Play*, p. 171.
5. *Baker's Dictionary of Theology*, "Repentance," by Karl Krominga (Grand Rapids: Baker Book House, 1960), p. 444.
6. H. S. Vigeveno, *Sinners Anonymous* (Waco: Word Books, 1970), p. 81.
7. Vigeveno, *Sinners Anonymous*, p. 83.
8. Berne, *Games People Play*, p. 48.
9. Berne, *Games People Play*, p. 184.
10. Anna Mow, *Going Steady with God* (Grand Rapids: Zondervan, 1970), pp. 30,31.

CHAPTER 8

1. Dennis Benson, *The Now Generation* (Richmond, Va.: John Knox Press, 1969), p. 31.
2. "Watch Out for False Spirituality" (Colossians Part 5), *Eternity*, April 1964, p. 27.
3. Maxwell Maltz, *Psycho-Cybernetics* (Essandes Special Editions, a Division of Simon & Schuster, Inc., New York: Prentice-Hall, Inc., 1960), p. 17.
4. Robert Schuller, *Move Ahead with Possibility Thinking* (New York: Doubleday & Company, 1967), pp. 32-34.
5. Keith Miller, *Habitation of Dragons* (Waco, Texas; Word Books, 1970.) see pp. 58-61.

CHAPTER 9

1. Larry Richards, *What's in It for Me?* (Chicago: Moody Press, 1970), p. 104.
2. Joseph Fletcher, *Situation Ethics: The New Morality* (Philadelphia: Westminster Press, 1966), pp. 36 and 55.
3. Concept of choosing between being an ethical thememoter or thermostat adapted from *The Way* (vol. 15, no. 3) 2850 Kalamazoo S. E.; Grand Rapids, Mich.
4. Fletcher, *Situation Ethics: The New Morality*, p. 71.
5. "Situation Morality: The Ethics of Immaturity," John Warwick Montgomery, EPA syndicated article, 1971. Montgomery's remarks were extracted from his debate with Joseph Fletcher at San Diego State College in February, 1971.
6. Myron Augsberger, *Faith for a Secular World* (Waco: Word Books, 1968), p. 39.

7. John Statt, "Christ: Lord and Liberator," *His magazine*, June 1971, p. 4.

8. Stott, "Christ: Lord and Liberator," p. 4.

9. See *The Letters to the Philippians, Colossians and Thessalonians*, William Barclay (Philadelphia: The Westminster Press, 1958), p. 180.

CHAPTER 10

1. Bernard Ramm, "What Makes a Man Spiritual?" (Colossians, Part 6), *Eternity*, May 1964, p. 29.

2. Barclay, *The Letters to the Philippians, Colossians and Thessalonians*, p. 188.

3. Robert Kistler, "Ten Year Old's Fourth Day as a Cub Scout Never Dawned," *Los Angeles Times*, February 13, 1971.

4. Paul Tournier, *The Meaning of Persons* (New York: Harper & Row, 1957).

5. John Powell, S.J., *Why Am I Afraid to Tell You Who I Am?* (Argus Communications Co., 1969).

CHAPTER 12

1. Italicized quotes reprinted by permission from "Rendezvous: a guide to a better quiet time," CAMPUS LIFE Magazine, April 1971. Copyright by Youth for Christ International, Wheaton, Illinois, p. 62.

2. Adapted from Rosalind Rinker's *Prayer: Conversing with God* (Grand Rapids: Zondervan, 1959), p. 50.

3. Excerpts from "Candle in My Heart," Cindy Randolph, from DECISION Magazine, © 1970 by The Billy Graham Evangelistic Assn.

4. Rinker, *Prayer: Conversing with God*, p. 43.

5. Rinker, *Prayer: Conversing with God*, p. 87.

6. Contributed to Rosalind Rinker's book *Prayer: Conversing with God* by Mrs. Vel Shearer, Mennonite youth group leader, pp. 90,91.

7. Adapted from *Prayer: Conversing with God*, p. 91.

8. Jimmy and Carol Owens, "Long Distance Love," from the musical *Show Me!* Published by John T. Benson Publishing Company, 1625 Broadway, Nashville, Tenn. Copyright 1971 by Lilleanas Publishing Company, 1971. All rights reserved. By permission.

9. Rinker, *Prayer: Conversing with God*, p. 23.

CONCLUSION

1. Larry Walker, minister at large, from the *Madison Baptist Church News Letter*.

2. Addison Leitch, "The Holy Spirit in These Days," copyright 1971 by *Christianity Today;* reprinted by permission.

3. Leitch, "The Holy Spirit in These Days," p. 15.